THE MAGNIFICENT
DEFEAT

THE MAGNIFICENT DEFEAT

Frederick Buechner

1817

Harper & Row, Publishers, San Francisco
Cambridge, Hagerstown, New York, Philadelphia
London, Mexico City, São Paulo, Singapore, Sydney

Grateful acknowledgment is made to the following publishers and authors for permission to use copyrighted material from the titles listed:

Harcourt, Brace & World, Inc.—T. S. Eliot, "Ash
Wednesday," *Collected Poems, 1909-1962*.

Harcourt, Brace & World, Inc.—James Weldon Johnson,
"The Creation." Used by permission of Will B.
Sandler, Esq.

Charles Scribner's Sons—Ernest Hemingway, *For Whom
the Bell Tolls*.

Union Seminary *Quarterly Review*—Frederick Buechner,
"A Christmas Triptych" (January 1964 issue);
reprinted here as "The Birth."

First Harper & Row paperback edition published in 1985.

Library of Congress Cataloging in Publication Data

Buechner, Frederick.
  The magnificent defeat.

  1. Meditations.   I. Title.
BV4832.2.B82   1985   242   84-48764
ISBN 0-06-061174-X (pbk.)

---

85 86 87 88 89 10 9 8 7 6 5 4 3 2

FOR JAMES MUILENBURG

Introductory Note

ALTHOUGH these meditations were originally presented to congregations composed largely of young people, I cannot excuse their shortcomings on the grounds that I was adapting my thought to the age of my listeners. In every case I said the most that I knew in the best way that I could at the moment when I was speaking, simplifying, where at all, only my language and the range of my illustrations.

As for theology, anyone in the least acquainted with the field will recognize my masters easily enough. Beyond them, I am peculiarly indebted, not only for what they taught me but for who they were, to James Muilenburg, to whom this book is dedicated, and also to George Buttrick, who was at a crucial time my pastor, and to John Knox and Paul Scherer, who were my teachers at Union Theological Seminary, and to Dean Robert Russell Wicks, who in many ways and over many years was my guide and friend.

Let the words of my mouth and the meditation of my heart be acceptable in thy sight, O Lord, my rock and my redeemer.

Contents

Introductory Note   6

Part I: THE CHALLENGE TO SURRENDER

The Magnificent Defeat   10
In the Beginning   19
The Power of God and
    the Power of Man   27
The Two Battles   36
Message in the Stars   44
Journey in Search of a Soul   51

Part II: THE TRIUMPH OF LOVE

The Annunciation   58
The Birth   66
The End Is Life   74
The Road to Emmaus   82
The Tiger   90
Follow Me   96
The Me in Thee   102

Part III: THE MYSTERY AND MIRACLE OF GRACE

The Breath of Life   110
To Be a Saint   116
The Breaking of Silence   124
Become like Children   131
The Miracles at Hand   136

Part I
THE CHALLENGE
TO SURRENDER

Be still, and know that I am God. Psalms 46:10 RSV

The Magnificent Defeat

The same night he arose and took his two wives, his two maids, and his eleven children, and crossed the ford of the Jabbok. He took them and sent them across the stream, and likewise everything that he had. And Jacob was left alone; and a man wrestled with him until the breaking of the day. When the man saw that he did not prevail against Jacob, he touched the hollow of his thigh; and Jacob's thigh was put out of joint as he wrestled with him. Then he said, "Let me go, for the day is breaking." But Jacob said, "I will not let you go, unless you bless me." And he said to him, "What is your name?" And he said, "Jacob." Then he said, "Your name shall no more be called Jacob, but Israel, for you have striven with God and with men, and have prevailed." Then Jacob asked him, "Tell me, I pray, your name." But he said, "Why is it that you ask my name?" And there he blessed him. So Jacob called the name of the place Peniel, saying, "For I have seen God face to face, and yet my life is preserved." The sun rose upon him as he passed Penuel, limping because of his thigh. Genesis 32:22–31 RSV

WHEN A MINISTER reads out of the Bible, I am sure that at least nine times out of ten the people who happen to be listening at all hear not what is really being read but only what they expect to hear read. And I think that what most people expect to hear read from the Bible is an edifying story, an uplifting thought, a moral lesson—something elevating, obvious, and boring. So that is exactly what very often they do hear. Only that is too bad because if you really listen—and maybe you have to forget that it is the Bible being read and a minister who is reading it—there is no telling what you might hear.

The story of Jacob at the river Jabbok, for instance. This stranger leaping out of the night to do terrible battle for God knows what reason. Jacob crying out to know his name but getting no answer. Jacob crippled, defeated, but clinging on like a drowning man and choking out the words, "I will not let you go, unless you bless me." Then the stranger trying to break away before the sun rises. A ghost, a demon? The faith of Israel goes back some five thousand years to the time of Abraham, but there are elements in this story which were already old before Abraham was born, almost as old as man himself. It is an ancient, jagged-edged story, dangerous and crude as a stone knife. If it means anything, what does it mean, and let us not assume that it means anything very neat or very edifying. Maybe there is more terror in it or glory in it than edification. But in any event, the place where you have to start is Jacob: Jacob the son of Isaac, the beloved of Rachel and Leah, the despair of Esau, his brother. Jacob, the father of the twelve tribes of Israel. Who and what was he?

An old man sits alone in his tent. Outside, the day is coming to a close so that the light in the tent is poor, but that is of no concern to the old man because he is virtually blind, and all he can make out is a brightness where the curtain of the tent is open to the sky. He is looking that way now, his head trembling under the weight of his great age, his eyes cobwebbed around with many wrinkles, the ancient, sightless eyes. A fly buzzes through the still air, then lands somewhere.

For the old man there is no longer much difference between life and death, but for the sake of his family and his family's destiny, there are things that he has to do before the last day comes, the loose ends of a whole long life to gather together and somehow tie up. And one of these in particular will not let him sleep until he has done it: to call his eldest son to him and give him his blessing, but not a blessing in our sense of the word—a pious formality, a vague expression of good will that we might use when someone is going on a journey and we say, "God bless you." For the old man, a blessing is the speaking of a word of great power; it is the conveying of something of the very energy and vitality of his soul to the one he blesses; and this final blessing of his firstborn son is to be the most powerful of all, so much so that once it is given it can never be taken back. And here even for us something of this remains true: we also know that words spoken in deep love or deep hate set things in motion within the human heart that can never be reversed.

So the old man is waiting now for his eldest son, Esau, to appear, and after a while he hears someone enter and say, "My father." But in the dark one voice sounds much like another, and the old man, who lives now only in the dark, asks, "Who are you, my son?" The boy lies and says that he is Esau. He says it boldly, and disguised as he is in Esau's clothes, and imitating Esau's voice—the flat, blunt tones of his brother—one can imagine that he is almost convinced himself that what he says is true. But the silence that follows his words is too silent, or a shadow falls between them—something—and the old man reaches forward as if to touch the face he cannot see and asks again, "Are you really my son, Esau?" The boy lies a second time, only perhaps not boldly now, perhaps in a whisper, perhaps not even bothering to disguise his voice in the half hope that his father will see through the deception. It is hard to know what the blind see and what they do not see; and maybe it was hard for the old man to distinguish clearly between what he believed and what he wanted to believe. But anyway, in the silence of his black goat-skin tent, the old man stretches out both of his arms and says, "Come near and kiss me, my son." So the boy comes near and kisses him, and the old man smells the smell of his garments and gives him the blessing, saying, "See, the smell of my son is the smell of a field which the Lord has blessed." The boy who thus by the most calculating stealth stole the blessing was of course Jacob, whose very name in Hebrew may mean "he who supplants," or, more colloquially translated, "the go-getter."

It is not, I am afraid, a very edifying story. And if you consider the aftermath, it becomes a great deal less edifying still. What I mean is that if Jacob, as the result of duping his blind old father, had fallen on evil times, if he had been ostracized by his family and friends and sent off into the wilderness somewhere to suffer the pangs of a guilty conscience and to repent his evil ways, then of course the moralists would have a comparatively easy time of it. As a man sows, so shall he reap. Honesty is the best policy. But this is just not the way that things fell out at all.

On the contrary. Once his dishonesty is exposed and the truth emerges, there is really surprisingly little fuss. Old Isaac seemed to take the news so much in his stride that you almost wonder if perhaps in some intuitive way he did not know that it had been Jacob all along and blessed him anyway, believing in his heart that he would make the worthier successor. Rebecca, the mother, had favored the younger son from the start, so of course there were no hard words from her. In fact only Esau behaved as you might have expected. He was furious at having been cheated, and he vowed to kill Jacob the first chance he got. But for all his raging, nobody apparently felt very sorry for him because the truth of the matter is that Esau seems to have been pretty much of a fool.

One remembers the story of how, before being cheated out of the blessing, he sold his birthright for some bread and some lentil soup simply because Jacob had come to him at a time when he was ravenously hungry after a long day in the fields—his birthright looking pale and intangible beside the fragrant reality of a good meal. So, although everybody saw that Esau had been given a raw deal, there seems to have been the feeling that maybe it was no more than what he deserved, and that he probably would not have known what to do with a square deal anyway.

In other words, far from suffering for his dishonesty, Jacob clearly profited from it. Not only was the blessing his, not to mention the birthright, but nobody seems to have thought much the worse of him for it, and there are no signs in the narrative that his conscience troubled him in the least. The only price he had to pay was to go away for a while until Esau's anger cooled down; and although one can imagine that this was not easy for him, he was more than compensated for his pains by the extraordinary thing that happened to him on his way.

For anyone who is still trying to find an easy moral here, this is the place to despair: because in the very process of trying to escape the wrath of the brother he had cheated, this betrayer of his father camped for the night in the hill country to the north, lay down with a stone for his pillow, and then dreamed not the nightmare of the guilty but a dream that nearly brings tears to the eyes with its beauty. The wonderful unexpectedness of it—of life itself, of God himself. He dreamed of a great ladder sct up on the earth with the top of it reaching into heaven and the angels ascending and descending upon it; and there above it in the blazing starlight stood the Lord God himself, speaking to Jacob words of great benediction and great comfort: "The land on which you lie I will give to your descendants, and your descendants will be like the dust of the earth, and behold, I am with you and will keep you wherever you go."

Do not misunderstand me about moralists. The ecclesiastical body to which I am answerable as a minister would, I am sure, take a rather dim view of it if I were to say, "Down with moralists!" but as a matter of fact that is neither what I want to say nor what I feel. Moralists have their point, and in the long run, and very profoundly too, honesty *is* the best policy. But the thing to remember is that one cannot say that until one has said something else first. And that something else is that, practically speaking, dishonesty is not a bad policy either.

I do not mean extreme dishonesty—larceny, blackmail, perjury, and so on—because practically speaking that is a bad policy if only on the grounds that either it lands the individual in jail or keeps him so busy trying to stay out of jail that he hardly has time to enjoy his ill-gotten gains once he has gotten them. I mean Jacob's kind of dishonesty, which is also apt to be your kind and mine. This is a policy that can take a man a long way in this world, and we are fools either to forget it or to pretend that it is not so.

This is not a very noble truth about life, but I think that it is a truth nonetheless, and as such it has to be faced just as in their relentless wisdom the recorders of this ancient cycle of stories faced it. It can be stated quite simply: the shrewd and ambitious man who is strong on guts and weak on conscience, who knows very well what he wants and directs all his energies toward getting it, the Jacobs of this world, all in all do pretty well. Again, I do not mean the criminal who is willing to break the law to get what he wants or even to take somebody's life if that becomes necessary. I mean the man who stays within the law and would never seriously consider taking other people's lives, but who from time to time might simply manipulate them a little for his own purposes or maybe just remain indifferent to them. There is no law against taking advantage of somebody else's stupidity, for instance. The world is full of Esaus, of suckers, and there is no need to worry about giving a sucker an even break because the chances are that he will never know what hit him anyway. In fact a sucker is by definition the man who never knows what hit him and thus keeps on getting hit—if not by us, by somebody else, so why not by us?

And the world is full of Isaacs, of people who cannot help loving us no matter what we do and whose love we are free to use pretty much as we please, knowing perfectly well that they will go on loving us anyway—and without really hurting them either, or at least not in a way that they mind, feeling the way they do. One is not doing anything wrong by all this, not in a way the world objects to, and if he plays it with any kind of sensitivity, a man is not going to be ostracized by anybody or even much criticized. On the contrary, he can remain by and large what the world calls a "good guy," and I do not use that term altogether ironically either. I mean "gooder" than many, good enough so that God in his infinite mercy can still touch that man's heart with blessed dreams.

Only what does it all get him? I know what you expect the preacher to say: that it gets him nothing. But even preachers must be honest. I think it can get him a good deal, this policy of dishonesty where necessary. It can get him the invitation or the promotion. It can get him the job. It can get him the pat on the back and the admiring wink that mean so much. And these, in large measure, are what we mean by happiness. Do not underestimate them.

Then it comes time for Jacob to go home again. He has lived long enough in the hill country to the north, long enough to marry and to get rich. He is a successful man and, as the world goes, a happy man. Old Isaac has long since died, and there is every reason to think that Esau is willing to let bygones be bygones. Good old Esau. Jacob wants to go home again, back to the land that God promised to Abraham, to Isaac, and now to him, as a gift. A gift. God's gift. And now Jacob, who knows what he wants and what he can get and how to get it, goes back to get that gift. And I mean *get*, and you can be sure that Jacob means it too.

When he reaches the river Jabbok, which is all that stands between him and the promised land, he sends his family and his servants across ahead of him, but he remains behind to spend the night on the near shore alone. One wonders why. Maybe in order to savor to its fullest this moment of greatest achievement, this moment for which all his earlier moments have been preparing and from which only a river separates him now.

And then it happens. Out of the deep of the night a stranger leaps. He hurls himself at Jacob, and they fall to the ground, their bodies lashing through the darkness. It is terrible enough not to see the attacker's face, and his strength is more terrible still, the strength of more than a man. All the night through they struggle in silence until just before morning when it looks as though a miracle might happen. Jacob is winning. The stranger cries out to be set free before the sun rises. Then, suddenly, all is reversed.

He merely touches the hollow of Jacob's thigh, and in a moment Jacob is lying there crippled and helpless. The sense we have, which Jacob must have had, that the whole battle was from the beginning fated to end this way, that the stranger had simply held back until now, letting Jacob exert all his strength and almost win so that when he was defeated, he would know that he was truly defeated; so that he would know that not all the shrewdness, will, brute force that he could muster were enough to get this. Jacob will not release his grip, only now it is a grip not of violence but of need, like the grip of a drowning man.

The darkness has faded just enough so that for the first time he can dimly see his opponent's face. And what he sees is something more terrible than the face of death—the face of love. It is vast and strong, half ruined with suffering and fierce with joy, the face a man flees down all the darkness of his days until at last he cries out, "I will not let you go, unless you bless me!" Not a blessing that he can have now by the strength of his cunning or the force of his will, but a blessing that he can have only as a gift.

Power, success, happiness, as the world knows them, are his who will fight for them hard enough; but peace, love, joy, are only from God. And God is the enemy whom Jacob fought there by the river, of course, and whom in one way or another we all of us fight—God, the beloved enemy. Our enemy because, before giving us everything, he demands of us everything; before giving us life, he demands our lives— our selves, our wills, our treasure.

Will we give them, you and I? I do not know. Only remember the last glimpse that we have of Jacob, limping home against the great conflagration of the dawn. Remember Jesus of Nazareth, staggering on broken feet out of the tomb toward the Resurrection, bearing on his body the proud insignia of the defeat which is victory, the magnificent defeat of the human soul at the hands of God.

In the Beginning

In the beginning God created the heavens and the earth. The earth was without form and void, and darkness was upon the face of the deep; and the Spirit of God was moving over the face of the waters. And God said, "Let there be light"; and there was light. And God saw that the light was good; and God separated the light from the darkness. God called the light Day, and the darkness he called Night. And there was evening and there was morning, one day. And God said, "Let there be a firmament in the midst of the waters, and let it separate the waters from the waters." And God made the firmament and separated the waters which were under the firmament from the waters which were above the firmament. And it was so. And God called the firmament Heaven. And there was evening and there was morning, a second day. And God said, "Let the waters under the heavens be gathered together into one place, and let the dry land appear." And it was so. God called the dry land Earth, and the waters that were gathered together he called Seas. And God saw that it was good. Genesis 1:1–10 RSV

THE AMERICAN POET James Weldon Johnson attempted in one of his poems to re-create some of the great power and sheer gorgeousness of an old-time Negro preacher's sermon on Creation.

And God stepped out on space,   2 1-2
And he looked around and said:
I'm lonely—
I'll make me a world.

19

And as far as the eye of God could see
Darkness covered everything,
Blacker than a hundred midnights
Down in a cypress swamp.

Then God smiled,
And the light broke,
And the darkness rolled up on one side
And the light stood shining on the other,
And God said: That's good!

Then God reached out and took the light in his hands,
And God rolled the light around in his hands
Until he made the sun;
And he set that sun a-blazing in the heavens.
And the light that was left from making the sun
God gathered it up in a shining ball
And flung it against the darkness,
Spangling the night with moon and stars.
Then down between
The darkness and the light
He hurled the world;
And God said: That's good.

I think that these lines serve their purpose well. They describe the Creation in the only language fit to describe it really, the language of poetry, which is a language made up of metaphors and music, of great intensity of feeling and great inventiveness. It is the language that man always uses when he tries to talk about the real mysteries of existence—the mysteries of love and death and beauty—and so it is of course also bound to be the language that he uses, that the wise man uses, when he tries to talk about the greatest mystery of all, including all the others, which is the mystery of life itself. What is life?

Everybody asks this one way or another, at one time or

another, and tries to answer it. Life is a rat race, we say, or a bed of roses, or not a bed of roses; or it is a battle to the death, a pain in the neck. This is the language of poetry too. Life is the flight of a bird that swoops out of the darkness of night into the great fire-lit hall of a castle. He wings his way wildly, batting against the walls, the ceiling, until finally he finds a window, then out into the darkness again. The first darkness is birth, the second is death, and in between—only for a few moments, a handful of years—the warmth, the sound of voices, the shadows cast by the fire.

One of my favorite definitions of life was spoken by a comic actress in some musical of years ago. "La vie, la vie!" she cried out, rolling her big, dark eyes. "We'd be dead without it!" And maybe that is all that we can say about it ever finally. Life is what we would be dead without. Life is what we are. Life is our little portion of Being itself. But that is only to define one mystery in terms of another. You and I and the most distant star and the dragonfly's wing and the rustle of leaves as they fall—these all have one thing in common, which is that they all *are*, we all are, part of Being. What is Being?

Think of this world. Think of the great globe itself, the cloud-capped towers, the gorgeous palaces, the solemn temples, and all the people of this world. Then take it all away, take the world itself away and us away so that not a rack is left behind. Think of the universe itself. Then take away all the planets and the stars, take away every form of matter and energy, take away space itself and take away time. What is left? All that one might say is left is the absence of all these things. Now take away this absence. Nothing is left. Non-Being. So Being is what we have instead of this. Your Being and mine, the Being of our world and of all the unseen

worlds. This is the great miracle. That Being *is*. It might
have *not* been. Where did it come from? Why?

We are not asking a scientific question now, and if I
tried to give a scientific answer, if I started talking in terms
of the Big Bang theory or the Steady State theory of the
origin of the universe—if, in other words, I tried to tell in
the language of science *how* everything got started, I would
leave you still unsatisfied because even if I could prove my
theory to be true, your question would go deeper than my
answer. It asks not what was the process by which Being
came to be, but what is the purpose. Not how was it created,
but why was it created. Who created it? Because that is the
way in which both poetry and religion finally ask it. Who?

If anyone says that is a pointless question because there
is no way of arriving at a definite answer, all one can reply
is that, be that as it may, one cannot help asking it even so,
if only because life keeps asking it of us. In a world where
at any moment the human race might be blown sky-high, our
lives ask us in the crudest and most relentless way possible
just this: Is life just a process that got started by some sort
of chemical accident and that will keep on going until some
damned fool comes along with a weapon that can destroy it
forever? Or is it something more than that?

To be honest, one has to admit that much of the immediate evidence points to the probability of the former.
And by and large, of course, that is where much of the
immediate evidence always points. Even in periods of com-
parative security and peace, the hard facts of death on the
one hand and of tragic mischance on the other quite power-
fully suggest that at the end of life, as at its beginning, there
is nothing but darkness—no creator, no creating word or spirit
moving over the face of the waters.

And yet: "In the beginning God created the heavens and the earth. . . . And God said, 'Let there be light. . . .'" And yet: "God stepped out on space, and he looked around and said, 'I'm lonely—I'll make me a world.'" There is always the poet, the lunatic, the lover; there is always the religious man who is a queer mixture of the three, all of them making their counter claims in a language and with a passion that not even the most skeptical among us are quite invulnerable to. And their strange, unsettling voices speaking to us from the inside and saying, "Yes, yes, but maybe after all, in the beginning and at the end there is . . . God, whoever he is, wherever he is."

Perhaps the only thing that anyone can be absolutely sure of is that he will never be able to prove it either way—with objective, verifiable proof. We can know that in the beginning there was God and not just some cosmic upheaval that brought light out of darkness only when we have experienced him doing the same thing in our lives, our world—bringing light out of our darkness.

To put it another way, unless there is some very real sense in which the Spirit of God moves over the dark and chaotic waters of this age, these deeps of yours and mine; unless God speaks his light- and life-giving word to me, then I do not really care much one way or the other whether he set the whole show spinning x billions of years ago. Unless I have some real experience of it myself, then even if someone could somehow prove to me objectively and verifiably that it all happened just as Genesis declares, I would be tempted to answer him with the two most devastating words in the English language: so what?

Does the Spirit of God move over the face of the turbulent waters of our age? The Hebrew word for "move" here

is *merahepeth,* which means to "brood" as a bird broods over
its nest until finally new life begins to stir beneath the shelter-
ing wings. Is new life stirring in this death-ridden world?
Is light about to be created out of our darkness? This is the
only question that matters.

However we answer it, one thing at least is beyond dis-
pute: we know in awful detail and with awful clarity just
how dark our history is. If there was a time when we could
look the other way and pretend that all was basically well,
for better or worse, that time has passed. We are familiar
with the dark things of our age to the point that we are really
obsessed by them. There is sometimes an almost lip-smacking
quality about our recital of them. So I have no heart for
running through the whole tragic catalogue now, and I should
think that in your hearts you would be grateful to me. I am
not asking you to look at the darkness of our times so much
as at the twilight of our times; I mean specifically at the
twilight of our gods.

The gods are dying. The gods of this world are sick unto
death. If someone does not believe this, the next time he
happens to wake up in the great silence of the night or of
the day, just listen. And after a while, at the heart of the
silence, he will hear the sound that gives it away: the soft,
crazy thud of the feet of the gods as they stagger across the
earth; the huge white hands fluttering like moths; the little
moans of bewilderment and anguish. And we all shudder at
the sound because to witness the death of gods is a fearsome
thing.

Which gods? The gods that we worship. The gods that
our enemies worship. Their sacred names? There is Science,
for one: he who was to redeem the world from poverty and
disease, on whose mighty shoulders mankind was to be borne

onward and upward toward the high stars. There is Communism, that holy one so terrible in his predilection for blood sacrifice but so magnificent in his promise of the messianic age: from each according to his ability, to each according to his need. Or Democracy, that gentler god with his gospel of freedom for all peoples, including those people who after centuries of exploitation and neglect at the hands of the older democracies can be set free now only to flounder in danger of falling prey to new exploiters. And we must not leave out from this role of the dying what often passes for the god of the church: the god who sanctifies our foreign policy and our business methods, our political views and our racial prejudices. The god who, bless him, asks so little and promises so much: peace of mind, the end of our inferiority complexes. Go to church and feel better. The family that prays together stays together. Not everybody can afford a psychiatrist or two weeks of solid rest in the country, but anybody can afford this god. He comes cheap.

These are the gods in whom the world has puts its ultimate trust. Some of them are our particular gods, and there are plenty of others, each can name for himself. And where are they now? They are dying, dying, and their twilight thickens into night. Where is the security that they promised? Where is the peace? The terrible truth is that the gods of this world are no more worthy of our ultimate trust than are the men who created them. Conditional trust, not ultimate trust.

And where are we? Stripped of our securities and bereft of our man-made gods, we stand as lonely and hypnotized spectators at the dance of death as it is being played out in our time. With the gods that we have created all going or gone, soon all that may remain is the God who created us, brooding over our darkness. He is awful in his majesty and power as he says, "Let there be light." He is more awful still in his love as he says, "I'm lonely—I'll make me a world."

I could stop now with a proclamation, that just as in the beginning he brought light out of darkness, so will the God of Creation bring light out of darkness again. And I could point to another even greater darkness that our world has known, when from the sixth hour to the ninth hour the sun was blotted out and a hideous cry was heard: *Eli, eli, lama sabachthani!* And I could proclaim with all the faith I have that out of that darkness came the most staggering light the world has known or will know. But instead of a proclamation, I will end with a question.

The former things are passing away and the gods are dying, just as the former things must pass away and the gods must die so that the new things can begin to come to life beneath the dark wings, so that creation can go on happening. My question is this: Are there in us, in you and me now, that recklessness of the loving heart, that wild courage, that crazy gladness in the face of darkness and death, that shuddering faithfulness even unto the end of the world, through which the new things can come to pass? Are there in us such qualities as these, which are in fact themselves the first glimmerings of the new things that even now are beginning to come to pass?

If not, God have mercy upon us, for we will soon be as yesterday when it is gone. If so, then we, even we, will have some part in the new heaven and the new earth that God is creating. By God's grace may it be so.

The Power of God and the Power of Man

And when they came to the disciples, they saw a great crowd about them, and scribes arguing with them. And immediately all the crowd, when they saw him, were greatly amazed, and ran up to him and greeted him. And he asked them, "What are you discussing with them?" And one of the crowd answered him, "Teacher, I brought my son to you, for he has a dumb spirit; and wherever it seizes him, it dashes him down; and he foams and grinds his teeth and becomes rigid; and I asked your disciples to cast it out, and they were not able." And he answered them, "O faithless generation, how long am I to be with you? How long am I to bear with you? Bring him to me." And they brought the boy to him; and when the spirit saw him, immediately it convulsed the boy, and he fell on the ground and rolled about, foaming at the mouth. And Jesus asked his father, "How long has he had this?" And he said, "From childhood. And it has often cast him into the fire and into the water, to destroy him; but if you can do anything, have pity on us and help us." And Jesus said to him, "If you can! All things are possible to him who believes." Immediately the father of the child cried out and said, "I believe; help my unbelief!" And when Jesus saw that a crowd came running together, he rebuked the unclean spirit, saying to it, "You dumb and deaf spirit, I command you, come out of him, and never enter him again." And after crying out and convulsing him terribly, it came out, and the boy was like a corpse; so that most of them said, "He is dead." But Jesus took him by the hand and lifted him up, and he arose. And when he had entered the house, his disciples asked

him privately, "Why could we not cast it out?" And he said to
them, "This kind cannot be driven out by anything but prayer."
They went on from there and passed through Galilee. And he
would not have anyone know it; for he was teaching his disciples,
saying to them, "The Son of man will be delivered into the hands
of men, and they will kill him. . . ."

Mark 9:14–31 RSV

IN THIS PASSAGE from Mark there are really two texts set side by side, yet because of the way the Bible is written—with no particular break in between, no change in style, just one verse following the other like beads on a string —partly just because of the way the Bible is printed on the page, it is easy to miss this and to see the whole passage as a single unit. But two texts there are, and they stand in the most violent sort of contrast with one another, a contrast that seems ironic even to the point of blasphemy. And the realities to which the two texts point are equally at odds, and the contrast between them is just as violent and ironic. Because the first text deals with the power of God and the second one deals with the power of man, and the printed page is almost torn in two by having to bear them both, just as this world is almost torn in two, just as you and I as individuals are almost torn in two, by having to contain them both. This is the great power struggle of our age and of all ages—not East against West, Communism against Democracy, White against Black, but this struggle: man's power against God's power, man against God and God against man.

The first part of the passage is a miracle story, and this, of course, is the power of God. It is not a very complicated story, but it is a little more complicated than it is apt to seem at first glance. Jesus finds his disciples in a very lively argument with a group of scribes, and a large crowd has gathered around to watch the fun. When Jesus asks what is going on, he finds out that a little while before, a man had come to the disciples to see if they could take his epileptic son and heal him. The disciples had tried to do this, and they had failed. So it was here that the scribes closed in to press home the point that must have been pretty obvious to everybody: hocus pocus. The hat with no rabbit in it. The sick boy had not even regained the power of speech. The crowd gathered. Even the father and his boy hung around too, God knows why.

And then, the narrative continues, Jesus came, and what happened at that point was not really very pretty or very pleasant, even though in the end a miracle was done. But it was not an easy business. You get the feeling that for everybody involved, it was a miracle that cost so much that if they had known the price in advance, it might never have happened.

The boy himself falls to the ground in the terrifying convulsions of epilepsy, yelping like an animal struck by a car, then lying there as if dead. His father, talking beforehand to Jesus, is confronted with certain deep things about himself that would cost any man pain—for one thing his utter inability in any way to help his own son, and, for another, the awful poverty of his faith· wanting so much to believe, to believe, but never quite being able to. And then the disciples —those poor, somehow characteristically inept men who throughout the Gospels seem to be always missing the point, always doing the wrong thing or failing to do the right thing, almost never being of much help to anybody, let alone to their Lord. They had tried themselves to heal the boy, but they had failed. And they stood there then and heard the man they followed speak words of great bitterness—words which revealed as much of his own pain, surely, as they must have added to theirs: "O faithless generation, how long am I to be with you? How long am I to bear with you?"

Then it happened, and very much as it had always happened before and continued to happen throughout his life. Almost two thirds of the Gospel narrative involves these stories of healing: nothing about Jesus is more certain historically than that he healed, however we want to understand it. We think of them all now—the lepers, the blind, the crippled, and the little girl who had died and his saying to her in Aramaic, "Talitha cumi!"—little girl, arise! And he does this again here, only now he does not say anything, just takes the unconscious boy by the hand, and lifts him, and then the boy gets up. The boy gets up.

This is text number one. The power of God. Text number two is about the power of man, and it can be stated very simply in the words that Jesus himself uses, speaking about himself: "The Son of man will be delivered into the hands of men, and they will kill him." This is the power of man.

Put them side by side, as close as we can, as close as we dare, and look sharp. The power of God. The power of man. The power of God in Jesus Christ—to heal, to give life; not to heal and give life only to the body, but to heal whatever is broken, to give life to whatever is dead, dying.

The power of man in the men who killed Jesus Christ, and it did not take great power either: a handful of soldiers, much less than a handful of nails, and reasonably strong stomachs on the part of the one or two men who actually did the job.

God's power. Man's power. Put them still closer together until they really start to crowd each other as in fact they really do; look at them even sharper if you can stand it. The power of God is powerless against the man who chooses to oppose it. In six hours or so the Son of God was just as dead as anybody else's son. The hands that healed the epileptic boy were just as ruined as any dead man's hands. And has God had any power in all the two thousand years that have gone by since? On the third day he rose again from the dead. This is the faith. But did he rise with power? Or did he rise the way the mist rises from the earth at daybreak—lovely, irrelevant, substanceless? Does God really have *power*?

Or is the power of God just the power of any great idea that man has in his head? Man has had many powerful ideas in his day—some good, some bad—and is God simply one of these ideas? Of course that would be to say that he is not really God at all, at least not in any sense that finally matters. And it would be to say too that such power as God does have will disappear entirely from this earth at the precise instant that there disappears also from this earth the last man who entertains God seriously as an idea.

If this is indeed all the power that God has—the power of an idea—then who in Hell is interested in him? In Hell —just there—who is interested in a God without power? Of course the answer is that everyone is: everyone is interested in a God without power, *interested*, and there is the end of it. In fact Hell might be described as the place or condition where men find God interesting and where this is all that they find; where they look at the Cross and are interested. And by this definition anyway, Hell is not altogether unfamiliar to any of us. How many preachers, for instance, make this their Sunday proclamation to the faithful: How interesting is God! How interesting to apply the idea of God to this and that, to the international situation, to family relations, or what have you. I shudder to think how often I have done it myself.

The power of God. Does he have any power? And I mean by power not just the power to make religiously inclined people feel cozy inside when they think about him. I mean power no less real and objective than the power in your body and mine to tear down a church stone by stone if we set our minds to it; no less objective and real than the power a doctor has to cure certain kinds of cancer; no less objective and real than the complexity of natural power that holds the planets in their courses and creates the capacity for vision in the spider's eye. Does God have *power*? What sort of power is it and where do we find it? Let me leave this question hanging and look at the power of man.

This does not take long—not that man has so little power that it is hardly worth mentioning, but that he has so much that it really does not need mentioning. Where do we begin even? I suppose we might begin by saying that man's most absolute power, the one that he can be surest of because it involves nothing except power, is his power to destroy. One does not need talent or brains to destroy. Anybody can do it: can destroy an animal, a bird, an object, an enemy or a friend, himself, Jesus Christ. There is no need to add that as matters stand now man has the power even to destroy mankind. However, that is only half the picture because in addition to his power to destroy, man also has the power to create. We can make things: paintings and political systems, theological systems, supersonic aircraft, iron lungs. In other words, the power of man consists of his ability to create and destroy for good or evil, but the one point I am interested in here is something else: that the fundamental characteristic of man's power, whatever form it takes, is that it tends to be external and coercive. It is fundamentally the power for better or worse to move things around—things and people and ideas. A man has power from the outside to push, pull, prod, and mold other men to his liking, for his good or for theirs, but it is only the outside of these other men that his power can affect.

A schoolteacher, for instance, has power to educate you, preach at you, befriend you, even make considerable sacrifices for you or ask you to make considerable sacrifices for him. But if any or all of these things is to affect anything deeper than just your conduct or your vocabulary, it will be not so much because of his power but in spite of it. Or one other example. Imagine a man invested with every form of human power that you can think of: the destructive power of a Hitler, the analytic power of a Freud, the creative power of a Shakespeare, the economic power of a J. Paul Getty, the moral and philanthropic power of a Schweitzer, and so on. Then try to imagine what he could do and what he could not do. He could conquer the world very likely, but could he satisfy the deepest longing of his own soul or your soul or mine? Could he satisfy the deepest longing of just one single human being out of all the millions that we can imagine his having conquered, and by "the deepest longing" I mean the longing for love, for deep peace, for meaning? I believe that he could not. This is something that no man has power to do either for himself or for anyone else. So in terms of what every man needs most crucially, all man's power is powerless because at its roots, of course, the deepest longing of the human soul is the longing for God, and this no man has the power to satisfy.

Here is a place to remember that for Christianity, the final affirmation about the nature of God is contained in the verse from the First Epistle of John: *God is love*. So another way of saying what I have just said is that man's deepest longing is for this love of God of which every conceivable form of human love is a reflection, however distorted a reflection it may be—"the smallest glass of love mixed with a pint pot of ditch-water," as Graham Greene says somewhere. And it is just for this reason that part of man's longing for the love of God can be satisfied simply by the love of man—the love of friend for friend, parent for child, sexual love—and thank God for that, literally thank him, because for many people human love is all there is, if that, because that is all they can believe in.

But notice this: that love is not really one of man's *powers*. Man cannot achieve love, generate love, wield love, as he does his powers of destruction and creation. When I love someone, it is not something that I have achieved, but something that is happening through me, something that is happening to me as well as to him. To use the old soap-opera cliché seriously, it is something bigger than both of us, infinitely bigger, because wherever love enters this world, God enters.

So the power of God stands in violent contrast with the power of man. It is not external like man's power, but internal. By applying external pressure, I can make a person do what I want him to do. This is man's power. But as for making him be what I want him to be, without at the same time destroying his freedom, only love can make this happen. And love makes it happen not coercively, but by creating a situation in which, of our own free will, we want to be what love wants us to be. And because God's love is uncoercive and treasures our freedom—if above all he wants us to love him, then we must be left free not to love him—we are free to resist it, deny it, crucify it finally, which we do again and again. This is our terrible freedom, which love refuses to overpower so that, in this, the greatest of all powers, God's power, is itself powerless.

Maybe some say, "I know human love, and I know something of its power to heal, to set free, to give meaning and peace, but God's love I know only as a phrase." Maybe others also say this, "For all the power that human love has to heal, there is something deep within me and within the people I know best that is not healed but aches with longing still. So if God's love is powerful enough to reach that deep, how do I find it? How?"

If that is really the question, if we are really seeking this power, then I have one thing to say—perhaps it is not the only thing, but it is enormously important: ask for it. There is something in me that recoils a little at speaking so directly and childishly, but I speak this way anyway because it is the most important thing I have in me to say. Ask, and you will receive. And there is the other side to it too: if you have never known the power of God's love, then maybe it is because you have never asked to know it—I mean really asked, expecting an answer.

I am saying just this: go to him the way the father of the sick boy did and ask him. Pray to him, is what I am saying. In whatever words you have. And if the little voice that is inside all of us as the inheritance of generations of unfaith, if this little voice inside says, "But I don't believe. I don't believe," don't worry too much. Just keep on anyway. "Lord, I believe; help my unbelief" is the best any of us can do really, but thank God it is enough.

Seek and you will find—this power of God's love to heal, to give peace and, at last, something like real life, so that little by little, like the boy, you can get up. Yes, get up. But we must seek—like a child at first, like playing a kind of game at first because prayer is so foreign to most of us. It is so hard and it is so easy. And everything depends on it. Seek. Ask. And by God's grace we will find. In Christ's name and with his power I can promise you this.

The Two Battles

Finally, be strong in the Lord and in the strength of his might. Put on the whole armor of God, that you may be able to stand against the wiles of the devil. For we are not contending against flesh and blood, but against the principalities, against the powers, against the world rulers of this present darkness, against the spiritual hosts of wickedness in the heavenly places. Therefore take the whole armor of God, that you may be able to withstand in the evil day, and having done all, to stand. Stand therefore, having girded your loins with truth, and having put on the breastplate of righteousness, and having shod your feet with the equipment of the gospel of peace; above all taking the shield of faith, with which you can quench all the flaming darts of the evil one. And take the helmet of salvation, and the sword of the Spirit, which is the word of God. Pray at all times in the Spirit, with all prayer and supplication.

Ephesians 6:10–18 RSV

ST. PAUL, or whoever it was who wrote this letter, was not the first to speak of life as a battle, nor was he the last; but familiar and hackneyed as the metaphor has become, it is also true. To grow, to move, to become, is to wage war against many adversaries. Most of the time it is an undeclared war. We do not announce publicly what we are fighting for or what we are fighting against or why we think that it is worth the fight, and very often we do not know the answer to these questions ourselves; but a kind of war is nonetheless what we are all engaged in, and the history of each individual no less than the history of nations rings loud with the tumult of it—advances and retreats, truces and delaying

36

actions, here a victory, there a defeat, all of it. Even in the silence of a church, for instance: the preacher advances, his tattered banners flying—maybe even God advances—and what do we do? Surrender? Retreat behind our shields? Launch some kind of counterattack of the heart, the mind? Who knows. But whatever we do, to live is to do battle under many different flags, and of all our battles, there are two, I believe, that are major ones.

The first is a war of conquest, which is a war to heat the blood of even the most timorous, because one way or another we all fight to conquer, and what we fight to conquer is the world. Not literally the world, perhaps, although like Walter Mitty we may dream a little in that direction sometimes; but for the most part our goal is a more realistic one: just a place in the world, a place in the sun, our place. And that takes fighting too, of course. All our lives we fight for a place in the sun—not a place in the shadows where we fear getting lost in the shadows and becoming a kind of shadow ourselves, obscure and unregarded. There are so many lives like that. We walk down the streets of a city—not just the poorer streets either—and the faces come at us like dead leaves in the wind, one face so much like another in its emptiness and defeat that it takes the most concentrated effort to see it as a human face at all, unique, individual, like the face of no other human being who has ever lived or will live. These are the invisible men of our world; we look at them without really seeing them. We fight to be *visible*, to move into a place in the sun, a place in the family, the community, in whatever profession we choose, a place where we can belong, where there is light enough to be recognized as a person and to keep the shadows at bay. The Germans use the word *lebensraum*, room to live in. We feel that we must conquer a territory in time and space that will be ours. And that is true. We must.

If that is the goal of this war of conquest that we all must wage, there are also the adversaries with whom we have to wage it; and they are adversaries of flesh and blood. They are human beings like ourselves, each of whom is fighting the same war toward the same end and under a banner emblazoned with the same word that our banners bear, and that word is of course Myself, or Myself and my Family, or Myself and my Country, Myself and my Race, which are all really MYSELF writ large. It can be the most ruthless of all wars, but on the other hand it need not be. Saints and sinners fight it both. Genghis Khan fought such a war under such a banner, but so does Martin Luther King. It can be the naked war of the jungle, my ambition against your ambition, my will against your will, or it can be war more in the sense of the knight at arms who abides by the rules of chivalry. If often it is the war of the unjust against the just, it can also be a war of the just against the unjust. But whichever it is, it is the war of flesh against flesh: to get ahead, to win, to gain or regain power, to survive in a world where not even survival is had without struggle.

To use the metaphor of Ephesians, what is the armor to wear in such a war? Not, certainly, the whole armor of God here but, rather, the whole armor of man, because this is a man's war against other men. In such a war, perhaps, you wear something like this. Gird your loins with wisdom, the sad wisdom of the world which knows that dog eats dog, that the gods help those who help themselves and charity begins at home. Put on the breastplate of self-confidence because if you have no faith in yourself, if you cannot trust to your own wits, then you will never get anywhere. Let your feet be shod with the gospel of success—the good news that you can get

just about anything in this world if you want it badly enough
and are willing to fight for it. Above all, take the shield of
security because in a perilous world where anything can happen, security is perhaps what you need more than anything
else—the security of money in the bank, or a college degree,
or some basic skill that you can always fall back on. And take
the helmet of attractiveness or personality and the sword of
wit. People are always criticizing the advertising business for
its implied promise that the one who gets the best job or the
prettiest girl is the one who wears the right clothes or uses
the right toothpaste or drinks the right brand of vodka. But
the fact of the matter is that although this is by no means a
happy truth about our society, it is nonetheless very often not
far from being true. In a world where the competition is
fierce, to dress well, to be able to speak well on your feet, to
be good at games, may actually make the difference between
winning and losing. In the war of conquest, that is to say, in
the war that we all wage for a place in the sun, it is the armor
of man rather than the armor of God that will serve you best;
and although I cannot value that armor as highly as some
would value it, I also cannot mock it because the armor of
man serves its purpose all too well, and because I wear some
of it myself, and so do you.

But there is another war that we fight, of course, all of
us, and this one is not a war against flesh and blood. "For
we are not contending against flesh and blood," the letter
reads. Then against what? What worse is there to contend
against in this world than other men? "The principalities
. . . the powers . . . the world rulers of this present darkness . . . the spiritual hosts of wickedness in the heavenly
places," Paul writes. "The wiles of the devil." This language
is so foreign to modern thinking and so offensive to modern

ears that when this famous passage is read at commencements and baccalaureates every year, I suspect that most people tend not really to hear it. They listen to the magnificent description of the whole armor of God that I have parodied and wrenched out of shape, and to the degree that they think about it at all, my guess is that they marvel at what stirring and beautiful words these are to address to the young as they prepare to step forth into the battle of life, and let it go at that.

But unless I am mistaken, the battle of life that they have in mind, and certainly the battle of life that most of the young have in mind, is the battle that I have tried to describe, the battle to get ahead. But in that battle, surely, the armor of God, which the letter catalogues, is not only of precious little use but will almost certainly prove an encumbrance. If any of us are battering our heads against the opposition of men, it is not the helmet of salvation that we need. If it is a higher place in the pecking order that we want, we can dispense with the sword of the Spirit. But what then is this other great war in which the armor of God, and only the armor of God, can see us through? What is this other great war that all of us wage in which it is the armor of man that becomes useless and sometimes worse than useless? There is no man, I believe, who does not know the answer.

This other war is the war not to conquer but the war to become whole and at peace inside our skins. It is a war not of conquest now but of liberation because the object of this other war is to liberate that dimension of selfhood which has somehow become lost, that dimension of selfhood that involves the capacity to forgive and to will the good not only of the self but of all other selves. This other war is the war to become a human being. This is the goal that we are really after and that God is really after. This is the goal that power, success, and security are only forlorn substitutes for. This is the victory that not all our human armory of self-confidence and wisdom and personality can win for us—not simply to be treated as human but to become at last truly human.

To describe our enemy in this war, the one that we must fight to liberate ourselves from, Paul writes of the devil—"the wiles of the devil"—and our age cringes at the word. But perhaps his word "darkness" will do. That is what we have to be set free from—the darkness in ourselves that we never fully see or fully understand or feel fully responsible for, although Heaven knows we are more than a little responsible. The science of psychology has its own vocabulary of darkness— trauma, psychosis, death-wish—but Paul says it so that a child could understand: "I do not do the good I want, but the evil I do not want is what I do." And it is also the evil in the world that the world does not want. No one but a madman, for instance, wants to blow up the world, but we live at a time when some of the sanest and wisest men on both sides of the iron curtain may decide to do just that. No one but a mad- man would will the mountains of the dead on the beaches of Normandy, at Auschwitz, Hiroshima, Vietnam, but there they lie. Call it what you will, the evil in this world is greater than the sum of all human evil, which is great enough, just as the evil in ourselves as individuals is greater than the evil that we choose, and that is great enough too. This is the darkness that we need to be liberated from in order to become human. This is what the great war of liberation is all about. "Wretched man that I am! Who will deliver me from this body of death?" This is the cry at the heart of every man and at the heart of the world.

It is for this war, not the other one, that we need the

whole armor of God. We must gird our loins with truth, and for us, in the end, there is only one truth, and it is the Christ. He is the truth about who man really is, about what it means to be really human, and about who God really is. And his Cross is the truth about what the darkness is, in us and in our world; and his Cross is the truth about what the love of God is, in us and in our world. We must put on the breast-plate of righteousness, and righteousness in the last analysis is love—not love as an emotion necessarily but love as an act of the will: love as the act of willing another's good even though we may despise the darkness in him just as we will our own good even though we despise the darkness in our-selves. It is not until we love a person in all his ugliness that we can make him beautiful, or ourselves either. Above all, we must take the shield of faith, and faith here is not so much believing this thing or that thing about God as it is hearing a voice that says, "Come unto me." We hear the voice, and then we start to go without really knowing what to believe either about the voice or about ourselves; and yet we go. Faith is standing in the darkness, and a hand is there, and we take it.

And finally, of course, we must "pray at all times in the Spirit . . . making supplication for all the saints and also for me." In the great war of liberation, it is imperative to keep in touch always with the only one who can liberate. We must speak to him however hard it may be in the thick of the fight, however irrelevant it may sometimes seem, however dried up and without faith we may feel. And we must not worry too much about the other war, the war of conquest. Of course to some extent we must worry about it, and it is necessary and right that we should. But in the war for a place in the sun, we must never mistake conquest for final victory, and above

all, we must never mistake failure for final defeat. Because
even if we do not find our place in the sun, or not quite the
place we want, or a place where the sun is not as bright as
we always dreamed that it would be, this is not the end because this is not really the decisive war even though we spend
so much of our lives assuming that it is. The decisive war is
the other one—to become fully human, which means to become compassionate, honest, brave. And this is a war against
the darkness which no man fights alone. It is the war which
every man can win who wills to win because it is the war
which God also wills us to win and will arm us to win if only
we will accept his armor.

Message in the Stars

Not that I have already obtained this or am already perfect; but I press on to make it my own, because Christ Jesus has made me his own. Brethren, I do not consider that I have made it my own; but one thing I do, forgetting what lies behind and straining forward to what lies ahead, I press on toward the goal for the prize of the upward call of God in Christ Jesus. . . . Therefore, my brethren, whom I love and long for, my joy and crown, stand firm thus in the Lord, my beloved. . . . Rejoice in the Lord always; again I will say, Rejoice. Let all men know your forbearance. The Lord is at hand. Have no anxiety about anything, but in everything by prayer and supplication let your requests be made known to God. And the peace of God, which passes all understanding, will keep your hearts and minds in Christ Jesus. Philippians 3:12—4:7 RSV

IF GOD REALLY EXISTS, why in Heaven's name does God not prove that he exists instead of leaving us here in our terrible uncertainty? Why does he not show his face so that at last a despairing world can have hope? At one time or another, everyone asks such a question. In some objectifiably verifiable and convincing way, we want God himself to demonstrate his own existence. Deep in our hearts, I suspect that this is what all of us want, unbelievers no less than believers. And I have wondered sometimes what would happen if God were to do just that. What would happen if God did set about demonstrating his existence in some dramatic and irrefutable way?

Suppose, for instance, that God were to take the great, dim river of the Milky Way as we see it from down here flowing across the night sky and were to brighten it up a little and then rearrange it so that all of a sudden one night the world would step outside and look up at the heavens and see not the usual haphazard scattering of stars but, written out in letters light years tall, the sentence: I REALLY EXIST, or GOD IS. If I were going to try to write a story or a play about such an event, I would start, of course, with the first night that this great theological headline appeared there in the stars, with suns and moons to dot the i's and the tails of comets to cross the t's. And I would try to show some of the ways that I can imagine people might respond to it. I would show some of them sinking to their knees, not because they are especially religious people but just because it might seem somehow the only natural thing to do under the circumstances. They would perhaps do it without even thinking about it, just crumpling down on their knees there in the tall grass out behind the garage. Some of them I would show running back into their houses in terror—guilty ones in terror of judgment, sophisticated ones in terror at the stark and terrible simplicity of it—just GOD IS written up there in the fire of the stars—and maybe in everyone some degree of terror at just the sheer and awesome vastness of the Unknown suddenly making itself known.

There would be a good many tears of regret, I suspect—people thinking that if only they had known it before, what different lives they might have had. And in many a person the sudden, wild upsurge of hope—the sick old man lying in bed where he cannot sleep and looking up through his bedroom window. On the table his clock ticktocks his time away, but there in the sky he sees proof at last of a reality beyond time. And I would want to touch at least on the peculiar astonishment of preachers and theologians who spend so much of their lives talking about God that unless they are very careful, God starts to lose all reality for them and to become just a subject for metaphysical speculation. For them too there would be this great affirmation in the night, and they would discover that they had been right after all, more right than perhaps they had ever quite been able to believe, and they would marvel at the strangeness of it.

What I would be trying to suggest in my story would be that the initial impact of God's supplying the world with this kind of objective proof of his existence would be extraordinary. Churches would have to overflow into football stadiums and open fields, wars would stop, crime would stop, a kind of uncanny hush would fall over the world. But as my story ended, I am afraid that in honesty I would have to suggest something else.

Several years would go by and God's proof of himself would still be blazing away every night for all to read. In order to convince people that the message was not just some million-to-one freak of nature, I would be tempted to have God keep on rewriting it in different languages, sometimes accompanying it with bursts of pure color or with music so celestial that finally the last hardened skeptic would be convinced that God must indeed exist after all. Then the way that I would have it end might be this. I would have a child look up at the sky some night, just a plain, garden-variety child with perhaps a wad of bubble gum in his cheek. If this were to be a movie, I would have a close-up here of just the child's eyes with the stars reflected in them, and I would have him spell out the message syllable by syllable. Let us say that this night it happens to be in French—*J'existe quand-même. C'est moi, le bon Dieu.* And deep in the heavens there would be the usual strains of sublime music. And then I would have the child turn to his father, or maybe, with the crazy courage of childhood, I would have him turn to God himself, and the words that I would have him speak would be words to make the angels gasp. "So what if God exists?" he would say. "Wl at difference does *that* make?" And in the twinkling of an eye the message would fade away for good and the celestial music would be heard no more, or maybe they would continue for centuries to come, but it would no longer make any difference.

We all want to be certain, we all want proof, but the kind of proof that we tend to want—scientifically or philosophically demonstrable proof that would silence all doubts once and for all—would not in the long run, I think, answer the fearful depths of our need at all. For what we need to know, of course, is not just that God exists, not just that beyond the steely brightness of the stars there is a cosmic intelligence of some kind that keeps the whole show going, but that there is a God right here in the thick of our day-by-day lives who may not be writing messages about himself in the stars but who in one way or another is trying to get messages through our blindness as we move around down here knee-deep in the fragrant muck and misery and marvel of the world. It is not objective proof of God's existence that we want but, whether we use religious language for it or not, the experience of God's presence. That is the miracle that we are really after. And that is also, I think, the miracle that we really get.

I believe that we know much more about God than we admit that we know, than perhaps we altogether know that we know. God speaks to us, I would say, much more often than we realize or than we choose to realize. Before the sun sets every evening, he speaks to each of us in an intensely personal and unmistakable way. His message is not written out in starlight, which in the long run would make no difference; rather it is written out for each of us in the humdrum, helter-skelter events of each day; it is a message that in the long run might just make all the difference.

Who knows what he will say to me today or to you today or into the midst of what kind of unlikely moment he will choose to say it. Not knowing is what makes today a holy mystery as every day is a holy mystery. But I believe that there are some things that by and large God is always saying to each of us. Each of us, for instance, carries around inside himself, I believe, a certain emptiness—a sense that something is missing, a restlessness, the deep feeling that somehow all is not right inside his skin. Psychologists sometimes call it anxiety, theologians sometimes call it estrangement, but whatever you call it, I doubt that there are many who do not recognize the experience itself, especially no one of our age, which has been variously termed the age of anxiety, the lost generation, the beat generation, the lonely crowd. Part of the inner world of everyone is this sense of emptiness, unease, incompleteness, and I believe that this in itself is a word from God, that this is the sound that God's voice makes in a world that has explained him away. In such a world, I suspect that maybe God speaks to us most clearly through his silence, his absence, so that we know him best through our missing him.

But he also speaks to us about ourselves, about what he wants us to do and what he wants us to become; and this is the area where I believe that we know so much more about him than we admit even to ourselves, where people hear God speak even if they do not believe in him. A face comes toward us down the street. Do we raise our eyes or do we keep them lowered, passing by in silence? Somebody says something about somebody else, and what he says happens to be not only cruel but also funny, and everybody laughs. Do we laugh too, or do we speak the truth? When a friend has hurt us, do we take pleasure in hating him, because hate has its pleasures as well as love, or do we try to build back some flimsy little bridge? Sometimes when we are alone, thoughts come swarming into our heads like bees—some of them destructive, ugly, self-defeating thoughts, some of them creative and glad. Which thoughts do we choose to think then, as much as we have the choice? Will we be brave today or a coward today? Not in some big way probably but in some little foolish way, yet brave still. Will we be honest today or a liar? Just some little pint-sized honesty, but honest still. Will we be a friend or cold as ice today?

All the absurd little meetings, decisions, inner skirmishes that go to make up our days. It all adds up to very little, and yet it all adds up to very much. Our days are full of nonsense, and yet not, because it is precisely into the nonsense of our days that God speaks to us words of great significance—not words that are written in the stars but words that are written into the raw stuff and nonsense of our days, which are not nonsense just because God speaks into the midst of them. And the words that he says, to each of us differently, are *be brave . . . be merciful . . . feed my lambs . . . press on toward the goal.*

But they are not all trivia and routine and nonsense, our lives. There are the crises too, crises that shake to the foundations both the great world of the nations and the little world of the individual. And we hear God speak through the crises too, many different kinds of words but sometimes, I think, a word quite different from the others. I am thinking of the great international crises that threaten the world itself with annihilation, and in terms of the individual, I am thinking of the deaths of people we love and of the failures and betrayals and of all that rises to imperil our inner peace.

In one of the last letters that St. Paul very likely ever wrote, a letter that he sent off from prison on his way to Rome and death, he has this to say at the end. "Rejoice in the Lord always; again I will say, Rejoice. The Lord is at hand. Have no anxiety about anything, but in everything by prayer and supplication with thanksgiving let your requests be known to God." And through the great crises of our times and through the little crises of each of our times, I believe that this is a deep part of what God says to us. Yes, take your times seriously. Yes, know that you are judged by the terrible sins of your times. Yes, you do well to faint with fear and foreboding at what is coming on the world. And yet rejoice. Rejoice. The Lord is at hand. Have no anxiety. Pray.

These words that God speaks to us in our own lives are the real miracles. They are not miracles that create faith as we might think that a message written in the stars would create faith, but they are miracles that it takes faith to see— faith in the sense of openness, faith in the sense of willingness to wait, to watch, to listen, for the incredible presence of God here in the world among us.

Journey in Search of a Soul

> Then Herod summoned the wise men secretly and ascertained from them what time the star appeared; and he sent them to Bethlehem, saying, "Go and search diligently for the child, and when you have found him bring me word, that I too may come and worship him." When they had heard the king they went their way; and lo, the star which they had seen in the East went before them, till it came to rest over the place where the child was. When they saw the star, they rejoiced exceedingly with great joy; and going into the house they saw the child with Mary his mother, and they fell down and worshiped him. Then, opening their treasures, they offered him gifts, gold and frankincense and myrrh. And being warned in a dream not to return to Herod, they departed to their own country by another way.
>
> Matthew 2:7–12 RSV

THINK ABOUT WHAT IT MEANS to be starting out on a journey, about what is really involved in being on our way. Of course, to begin with, we just put one foot ahead of the other foot, leg over leg, and our steps make a little thud as they carry us farther and farther down the road. Then we probably climb into a car or a train or a plane, and then the miles begin to go by a lot faster, and soon we look around, and the place that we have left has disappeared entirely, and the place where we are going still lies off in the distance somewhere, and there we are somewhere in between. It is really a strange sort of state to be in, not quite like anything else.

For instance, the most real thing there is for us then is the journey itself, and not only the place that we left but even the place where we are going become almost dreamlike by comparison, even though they may be the places that we know best in the world. What is real is the ache in our arms and shoulders as we lug our baggage from one station to another. What is real is the stranger with no eyes who is waiting there at the street corner for somebody to come along and tell him when the light has changed. What is real is the way our hearts leap into our throats when suddenly it begins snowing and all in a minute we know that the world is really a beautiful place after all and that life is good beyond all telling, and the little boy standing near us sticks out his tongue and lets a snowflake melt on it.

When we are on a journey, what is real is not so much the role we play, the mask we wear, in the place that we are leaving, and not even the roles we will soon be called on to play when we get to the place where we are going. Instead, what becomes increasingly real as we travel along is something much closer to the actual face that lies behind all the masks and that gives a kind of relative unity to all the different parts that our life demands that we play. In other words, travel can be a very unmasking experience, bringing us suddenly face to face with ourselves—as when we are gazing out of a train window at the endless line of telegraph poles whipping by, and we find that part of what we are looking at is our own reflection.

And it can be unmasking in another way too, I think, because when we are moving through that no-man's land, that everyman's land, between worlds, there is no one around to hold us to any particular form of conduct or even to look to us to behave in a way consistent with the way that we have usually behaved in the past. And the result of this is that to an extraordinary extent we are free to do whatever we like, and the result of this is that what you do is apt to be a more accurate definition than usual of who you really are.

The blind stranger waits at the corner for someone to tell him when the light has changed—or God only knows what the blind stranger is waiting there for, maybe he's waiting even for you—and whatever you do then or do not do, just that is apt to be precisely who you are. "You break my heart, stranger without any eyes," you may say, "but it's already late, and I have miles to go before I sleep." Or, "Stranger who is not a stranger, we both in our own ways labor and are heavy-laden. Let us bear each other's burdens." Or what?

I speak of journeys because of course we are all of us on a journey ourselves. The comparison of life to a road is a very ancient one, and you and I are travelers along that road whether we think of it that way or not, traveling from the unknown into the unknown. I think of the three wise men from the East setting off on their journey and traveling many a long and weary mile with their strange gifts before they finally reach the place where the star stands still. And because what they found when they reached that place was a child, and because it is toward the birth of that same child that our world is traveling again now as December day follows December day—because of these things I think of one of the great stories written for children, which itself tells of a journey that a child took with three outlandish companions, a story from which I believe there is much to learn about all our journeys, especially the journey that begins with Advent and ends, if you can say it ends, with Christmas.

Needless to say I am referring to L. Frank Baum's *The*

Wizard of Oz, which seems to me not only the greatest fairy tale that this nation has produced but one of its great myths. Caught up in the vortex of a Kansas cyclone, a child named Dorothy is blown away to the Land of Oz, which is a strange and beautiful place but which she knows that she must leave in order to return to her home in Kansas. The only one who can help her to return is the great Wizard of Oz himself, and so she sets off for the Emerald City to find him. On her way, she is joined by three remarkable creatures, each of whom has his own favor to ask of the wizard. The first is a Scarecrow, who wants a brain more than anything else. The second is a Tin Woodman, who yearns for a heart. The third is a Cowardly Lion, who is searching, of course, for courage. I will not try to describe all the things that happen on their journey except to say that in the manner of fairy tales, most of them are pretty hair-raising, yet somehow they finally come through. Only how do they come through?

In a rather unexpected way, really, because whenever they are confronted with some sort of physical danger, for instance, it is always the Cowardly Lion who somehow manages to fight their way out of it. Whenever the obstacle is of a more cerebral nature, it is always the brainless Scarecrow who figures out a way to circumvent it. And as for the Tin Woodman, who is journeying in search of a heart, although he lends a hand whenever he can, very often he tends to be more of a hindrance than a help because he is so given to being moved by the plight of others that everyone keeps having to rally around him with an oilcan to make sure that his tears do not rust him. The climax of the tale occurs when, upon reaching the Emerald City at last, they make the shattering discovery that the great wizard is not really great at all, not really even a wizard. He is a rather helpless little

man with a bald head who says himself that he is a humbug
and that he cannot possibly grant the requests of this little
band that has journeyed to him from so far. Yet is this entirely true? Is he really a humbug? Is he really unable to
give them what they want?

What he does is to point out that each of them already
has what he traveled such a distance to find. And here we
have to listen carefully, because here the fairy tale becomes
something more than a fairy tale and the journey down the
Yellow Brick Road becomes a journey of more than just a
Cowardly Lion, a Tin Woodman, and a Scarecrow. Because
what the helpless little man who is not and yet really is a
wizard says to them is, in effect, that things like a brain, a
heart, and courage are never had as gifts, but are always
earned.

This seems so obvious in a way that we would think one
would have to be a Scarecrow not to see it, but that is not so.
We want very much what these three wanted, and that is to
become fully men, to become fully persons. And we want
it for the same reason that they wanted it, because as things
stand now we know that we are only partly men, partly persons. Like them again, we expect that what we want will
simply happen to us one day, by some sort of wizardry. We
all tend to say something like this: "I am not now altogether
the person I wish I were—my heart is less than a man's heart
should be, all shut off behind tin; my brain is a thing stuffed
full of the straw of other people's ideas; and courage? There
are times when I don't even have the courage to face myself.
I am not the man I would like to be, but someday I will
become that man. When things straighten out. When all
the pressures on me let up a little. When I grow up. But
the hard truth is that this day may never come, and for many

who grew up years ago it has never come simply because they did not understand that courage is his who with his scalp cold with fear yet acts courageously. A brain, a real brain, is his who knows that he is as much a fool as a Scarecrow yet manages somehow to do all that a Scarecrow can. A heart is his who is willing to let it be broken. For us, at Christmastime, the one who confronts us with ourselves and with this truth is not a wizard who is a humbug but God who is a child.

As for the little girl named Dorothy, she was intact as a human being and therefore not in the same kind of need as her strange companions. But at the same time she was lost, and her great need was somehow to get back home. She did not know how she could get back, but there was one thing that she did know, and it was of crucial importance: home for her was not the Land of Oz for all its loveliness. Home was instead her uncle's farm, on the prairie, where life was not easy and cyclones often darkened the sky.

So, too, home for the three wise men and for us is not the manger where the light is gentle and God is a child. Peace is there, the peace that passes all understanding, but it is not to be ours yet for a while. We also must depart into our own country again, where peace is not found in escape from the battle but in the very heat of the battle. For outlandish creatures like us, on our way to a heart, a brain, and courage, Bethlehem is not the end of our journey but only the beginning—not home but the place through which we must pass if ever we are to reach home at last.

Part II
THE TRIUMPH
OF LOVE

Behold, the Lamb of God,
who takes away the sin of the world!
John 1:29 RSV

The Annunciation

*In the sixth month the angel Gabriel was sent
from God to a city of Galilee named Nazareth, to a virgin betrothed to a man whose name was Joseph, of the house of David;
and the virgin's name was Mary. And he came to her and said,
"Hail, O favored one, the Lord is with you!" But she was greatly
troubled at the saying, and considered in her mind what sort of
greeting this might be. And the angel said to her, "Do not be
afraid, Mary, for you have found favor with God. And behold,
you will conceive in your womb and bear a son, and you shall
call his name Jesus.*

*He will be great, and will be called the Son of the Most
    High;*
*and the Lord God will give to him the throne of his father
    David,*
and he will reign over the house of Jacob for ever;
and of his kingdom there will be no end."

*And Mary said to the angel, "How can this be, since I have
no husband?" And the angel said to her,*
"The Holy Spirit will come upon you,
and the power of the Most High will overshadow you;
therefore the child to be born will be called holy,
the Son of God."

Luke 1:26–35 RSV

"IN THE SIXTH MONTH the angel Gabriel was
sent from God to a city of Galilee named Nazareth, to a
virgin betrothed to a man whose name was Joseph, of the
house of David; and the virgin's name was Mary," and that
is the beginning of a story—a time, a place, a set of char-
acters, and the implied promise, which is common to all

stories, that something is coming, something interesting or
significant or exciting is about to happen. And I would
like to start out by reminding my reader that in essence this
is what Christianity is. If we whittle away long enough, it
is a story that we come to at last. And if we take even the
fanciest and most metaphysical kind of theologian or preacher
and keep on questioning him far enough—Why is this so?
All right, but why is *that* so? Yes, but how do we know that
it's so?—even he is forced finally to take off his spectacles
and push his books off to one side and say, "Once upon a
time there was . . . ," and then everybody leans forward a
little and starts to listen. Stories have enormous power for
us, and I think that it is worth speculating why they have
such power. Let me suggest two reasons.

One is that they make us want to know what is coming
next, and not just out of idle curiosity either because if it is a
good story, we *really* want to know, almost fiercely so, and
we will wade through a lot of pages or sit through a lot of
endless commercials to find out. There was a young woman
named Mary, and an angel came to her from God, and what
did he say? And what did she say? And then how did it all
turn out in the end? But the curious thing is that if it is a
good story, we want to know how it all turns out in the end
even if we have heard it many times before and know the
outcome perfectly well already. Yet why? What is there to
find out if we already know?

And that brings me to the second reason why I think
stories have such power for us. They force us to consider
the question, "Are stories true?" Not just, "Is *this* story
true?"—was there really an angel? Did he really say, "Do not
be afraid"?—but are any stories true? Is the claim that all
stories make a true claim? Every storyteller, whether he is

Shakespeare telling about Hamlet or Luke telling about Mary,
looks out at the world much as you and I look out at it and
sees things happening—people being born, growing up, working, loving, getting old, and finally dying—only then, by the
very process of taking certain of these events and turning
them into a story, giving them form and direction, does he
make a sort of claim about events in general, about the
nature of life itself. And the storyteller's claim, I believe, is
that life has meaning—that the things that happen to people
happen not just by accident like leaves being blown off a
tree by the wind but that there is order and purpose deep
down behind them or inside them and that they are leading
us not just anywhere but somewhere. The power of stories
is that they are telling us that life adds up somehow, that
life itself is like a story. And this grips us and fascinates us
because of the feeling it gives us that if there is meaning in
any life—in Hamlet's, in Mary's, in Christ's—then there is
meaning also in our lives. And if this is true, it is of enormous
significance in itself, and it makes us listen to the storyteller
with great intensity because in this way all his stories are
about us and because it is always possible that he may give
us some clue as to what the meaning of our lives is.

The story that Christianity tells, of course, claims to
give more than just a clue, in fact to give no less than the
very meaning of life itself and not just of some lives but of
all our lives. And it goes a good deal further than that in
claiming to give the meaning of God's life among men, this
extraordinary tale it tells of the love between God and man,
love conquered and love conquering, of long-lost love and
love that sometimes looks like hate. And so, although in one
sense the story Christianity tells is one that can be so simply
told that we can get the whole thing really on a very small

Christmas card or into the two crossed pieces of wood that
form its symbol, in another sense it is so vast and complex
that the whole Bible can only hint at it. Where does the
story of God and man begin, for instance? Biblically speaking, you would have to say that it begins with Genesis and
the picture we get of the Spirit of God brooding over the
dark waters of chaos before the great "Let there be light!" of
Creation sounded. But that amounts to saying that it has no
beginning in time at all. Or where do we say that it ends?
With the Crucifixion perhaps, where man brings the story
to an end by killing God, or with nuclear war perhaps, where
man brings it to an end by killing himself. But the answer to
this is, "Behold, I create new heavens and a new earth!" and
"He that believeth in me, though he were dead, yet shall he
live," so the Christian story is beyond time altogether.

Yet it is also in time, the story of the love between
God and man. There is a time when it begins, and therefore
there is a time before it begins, when it is coming but not
yet here, and this is the time Mary was in when Gabriel
came to her. It is Advent: the time just before the adventure
begins, when everybody is leaning forward to hear what will
happen even though they already know what will happen
and what will not happen, when they listen hard for meaning,
their meaning, and begin to hear, only faintly at first, the
beating of unseen wings.

The angel said to her, " 'Hail, O favored one, the Lord
is with you!' But she was greatly troubled at the saying, and
considered in her mind what sort of greeting this might be."
And well she might have been troubled if she had any idea
of what lay ahead for her and her baby, and to one degree
or another we must believe that she did. In the great medieval
paintings of the scene, the Annunciation, the air is painted

in gold leaf, and the figures of Mary and Gabriel stand there as still as death. There is no movement. None. Even the robe of the angel, still billowed out by the winds of Heaven, is frozen, and so is the wind itself. Time itself seems to have stopped. It is a moment beyond time. And of course there is truth in these ancient paintings because when our vision of the world suddenly deepens and brightens—when we suddenly see an angel where before we saw only empty space, when in a flash of light we have the uncanny sense that our lives are not just happening to us but are trying to tell us something of unspeakable importance—then for a moment we are stunned. We are stopped dead in our tracks, and the whole world holds its breath, and even the air becomes as rich and impenetrable as gold. But that is only part of the truth, because when angels draw near, as they do, the earth begins to shake beneath our feet as it began to shake beneath Mary's feet, which was why she was greatly troubled. Instead of everything standing still and sure, suddenly nothing is standing still, and everything is unsure. Something new and shattering is breaking through into something old. Something is trying to be born. And if the new thing is going to be born, then the old thing is going to have to give way, and there is agony in the process as well as joy, just as there is agony in the womb as it labors and contracts to bring forth the new life.

But this is the language of poetry, and I use it because it is the language in which the Annunciation is described and the only language in which it can be described. But there are other languages to describe other things. How, for instance, do you describe this world of ours in revolution, a world beneath whose oceans at this moment an American atomic submarine is cruising armed with missiles whose explosive power exceeds that of all the bombs set off in the two world wars? What is trying to happen? Something is trying to happen, we can be sure of that, and the earth is shaking beneath our feet at its approach.

Men have seen something; the Communists have seen it no less clearly than we and in some ways perhaps more clearly. And what men have seen is something that has never existed anywhere in history and exists nowhere today except in their vision of it: a world where men live together as brothers. "No more shall there be in it an infant that lives but a few days, or an old man who does not fill out his days. They shall not labor in vain, or bear children for calamity. The wolf and the lamb shall feed together, the lion shall eat straw like the ox; and dust shall be the serpent's food. They shall not hurt or destroy in all my holy mountain, says the Lord."

These are Isaiah's words for it, the words of poetry again. But it is the same world that Communism is talking about in the words of Marxian economic theory, the same world that the Western Alliance is talking about in the words of Christian Democracy, a world that never was on land or sea but a world that is pressing in upon us through our vision of it. So what do the nations do? Two things at once, I think, and things that contradict each other and are always at war. On the one hand, they are trying to materialize the vision, to bring it about. The tools they use are the weapons they have forged in their factories and the political and economic ideas they have forged in their heads. The price that they are all but willing to pay for it is death because there are times when even death seems not too high a price to pay for life, new life. And yet at the same time, and with the same tools, they are trying to prevent its being brought about, to bring about instead not the world of their vision but a man-made version of it, a more reasonable and less demanding facsimile where the serpent gets a little more than dust to eat, and the lion is allowed an occasional taste of blood. We try to fend off this world we yearn for where men live together as brothers because there is something in each of us that wants to live not for his brother but for himself. We fend it off because we know in our terrible wisdom that the price we must pay for it *is* death, the death of self and all the values of self, the death that must take place before the life can come.

In an odd way it is so comforting to talk about history, even the tragic history of our own times, because it is so much *out there* somewhere, outside these walls, beyond the town limits, across the river. And all the wars and the threats of war are out there too, and with them the strange thing which is not an angel because we believe there are no angels but which is something of great terror and great beauty gathering to a brightness. The world waits. History waits and labors. Something draws near, and we love its being far away there rather than here, among ourselves. Except, of course, that it is here among us too and within us as we wait for the story to begin, the story whose end we already know and yearn to know again and wish we did not know: the story whose meaning may be our meaning, as we wait for the child to be born.

For this is what Gabriel comes to announce, and Mary stands there as still as life in her blue mantle with her hands folded on her lap, and the terrible salutation is caught like a bird's wing in the golden net of the air—*Ave Maria gratia plena. Dominus tecum.* And then she hears him say, "Behold, you will conceive in your womb and bear a son, and

you shall call his name . . . ." But she knows his name before Gabriel says it, just as we also know his name, because
the child who is going to be born is our child as he is her
child. He is that which all the world's history and all of our
own inner histories have been laboring to bring forth. And
it will be no ordinary birth but a virgin birth because the
birth of righteousness and love in this stern world is always
a virgin birth. It is never men nor the nations of men nor
all the power and wisdom of men that bring it forth but always God, and that is why the angel says, "The child to be
born will be called the Son of God."

Here at the end let me tell a story which seems to me
to be a kind of parable of the lives of all of us. It is a peculiarly twentieth-century story, and it is almost too awful to
tell: about a boy of twelve or thirteen who, in a fit of crazy
anger and depression, got hold of a gun somewhere and fired
it at his father, who died not right away but soon afterward.
When the authorities asked the boy why he had done it, he
said that it was because he could not stand his father, because
his father demanded too much of him, because he was always after him, because he hated his father. And then later
on, after he had been placed in a house of detention somewhere, a guard was walking down the corridor late one night
when he heard sounds from the boy's room, and he stopped
to listen. The words that he heard the boy sobbing out in
the dark were, "I want my father, I want my father."

Our father. We have killed him, and we will kill him
again, and our world will kill him. And yet he is there. It
is he who listens at the door. It is he who is coming. It is
our father who is about to be born. Through Jesus Christ
our Lord.

The Birth

THE INNKEEPER

And she gave birth to her first-born son and wrapped him in swaddling cloths, and laid him in a manger, because there was no place for them in the inn.   Luke 2:7 RSV

"THAT WAS A LONG, LONG TIME AGO," said the Innkeeper, "and a long, long way away. But the memories of men are also long, and nobody has forgotten anything about my own sad, queer part in it all unless maybe they have forgotten the truth about it. But you can never blame people for forgetting the truth because it is, after all, such a subtle and evasive commodity. In fact, all that distinguishes a truth from a lie may finally be no more than just the flutter of an eyelid or the tone of a voice. If I were to say, 'I BELIEVE!' that would be a lie, but if I were to say, 'I believe . . .' that might be the truth. So I do not blame posterity for forgetting the subtleties and making me out to be the black villain of the piece—the heartless one who said, 'No room! No room!' I'll even grant you that a kind of villainy may be part of the truth. But if you want to speak the whole truth, then you will have to call me a villain with a catch in your voice, at least a tremor, a hesitation maybe, with even the glitter of almost a tear in your eye. Because nothing is entirely black, you know. Not even the human heart.

"I speak to you as men of the world," said the Innkeeper. "Not as idealists but as realists. Do you know what it is like to run an inn—to run a business, a family, to run anything in this world for that matter, even your own life? It is like being lost in a forest of a million trees," said the Innkeeper, "and each tree is a thing to be done. Is there fresh linen on all the beds? Did the children put on their coats before they went out? Has the letter been written, the book read? Is there money enough left in the bank? Today we have food in our bellies and clothes on our backs, but what can we do to make sure that we will have them still tomorrow? A million trees. A million things.

"Until finally we have eyes for nothing else, and whatever we see turns into a thing. The sparrow lying in the dust at your feet—just a thing to be kicked out of the way, not the mystery of death. The calling of children outside your window—just a distraction, an irrelevance, not life, not the wildest miracle of them all. That whispering in the air that comes sudden and soft from nowhere—only the wind, the wind. . . .

"Of course I remember very well the evening they arrived. I was working on my accounts and looked up just in time to see the woman coming through the door. She walked in that slow, heavy-footed way that women have in the last months, as though they are walking in a dream or at the bottom of the sea. Her husband stood a little behind her— a tongue-tied, helpless kind of man, I thought. I cannot remember either of them saying anything, although I suppose some words must have passed. But at least it was mostly silence. The clumsy silence of the poor. You know what I mean. It was clear enough what they wanted.

"The stars had come out. I remember the stars perfectly though I don't know why I should, sitting inside as I was. And my wife's cat jumped up onto the table where I was sitting. I had not stood up, of course. There was mainly just silence. Then it happened much in the way that you have heard. I did not lie about there being no room left—there really was none—though perhaps if there had been a room, I might have lied. As much for their sakes as for the sake of the inn. Their kind would have felt more at home in a stable, that's all, and I do not mean that unkindly either. God knows.

"Later that night, when the baby came, I was not there," the Innkeeper said. "I was lost in the forest somewhere, the unenchanted forest of a million trees. Fifteen steps to the cellar, and watch out for your head going down. Firewood to the left. If the fire goes out, the heart freezes. Only the wind, the wind. I speak to you as men of the world. So when the baby came, I was not around, and I saw none of it. As for what I heard—just at that moment itself of birth when nobody turns into somebody—I do not rightly know what I heard.

"But this I do know. My own true love. All your life long, you wait for your own true love to come—we all of us do—our destiny, our joy, our heart's desire. So how am I to say it, gentlemen? When he came, I missed him.

"Pray for me, brothers and sisters. Pray for the Innkeeper. Pray for me, and for us all, my own true love."

THE WISE MAN

> Now when Jesus was born in Bethlehem of Judea in the days of Herod the king, behold, wise men from the East came to Jerusalem, saying, "Where is he who has been born king of the Jews? For we have seen his star in the East, and have come to worship him."

> Matthew 2:1–2 RSV

"'BEWARE OF BEAUTIFUL STRANGERS,'" said one of the magi-astrologers, the wise men, "and on Friday avoid travel by water. The sun is moving into the house of Venus so affairs of the heart will prosper.' We said this to Herod, or something along those lines, and of course it meant next to nothing. To have told him anything of real value, we would have had to spend weeks of study, months, calculating the conjunction of the planets at the precise moment of his birth and at the births of his parents and their parents back to the fourth generation. But Herod knew nothing of this, and he jumped at the nonsense we threw him like a hungry dog and thanked us for it. A lost man, you see, even though he was a king. Neither really a Jew nor really a Roman, he was at home nowhere. And he believed in nothing, neither Olympian Zeus nor the Holy One of Israel, who cannot be named. So he was ready to jump at anything, and he swallowed our little jingle whole. But it could hardly have been more obvious that jingles were the least of what he wanted from us.

"'Go and find me the child,' the king told us, and as he spoke, his fingers trembled so that the emeralds rattled together like teeth. 'Because I want to come and worship him,' he said, and when he said that, his hands were still as death. Death. I ask you, does a man need the stars to tell him that no king has ever yet bowed down to another king? He took us for children, that sly, lost old fox, and so it was like children that we answered him. 'Yes, of course,' we said, and went our way. His hands fluttered to his throat like moths.

"Why did we travel so far to be there when it happened? Why was it not enough just to know the secret without having to be there ourselves to behold it? To this, not even the stars had an answer. The stars said simply that he would be born. It was another voice altogether that said to go—a voice as deep within ourselves as the stars are deep within the sky.

"But why did we go? I could not tell you now, and I could not have told you then, not even as we were in the very process of going. Not that we had no motive but that we had so many. Curiosity, I suppose: to be wise is to be eternally curious, and we were very wise. We wanted to see for ourselves this One before whom even the stars are said to bow down—to see perhaps if it was really true because even the wise have their doubts. And longing. Longing. Why will a man who is dying of thirst crawl miles across sands as hot as fire at simply the possibility of water? But if we longed to receive, we longed also to give. Why will a man labor and struggle all the days of his life so that in the end he has something to give the one he loves?

"So finally we got to the place where the star pointed us. It was at night. Very cold. The Innkeeper showed us the way that we did not need to be shown. A harebrained, busy man. The odor of the hay was sweet, and the cattle's breath came out in little puffs of mist. The man and the woman. Between them the king. We did not stay long. Only a few minutes as the clock goes, ten thousand, thousand years. We set our foolish gifts down on the straw and left.

"I will tell you two terrible things. What we saw on the face of the new-born child was his death. A fool could have seen it as well. It sat on his head like a crown or a bat, this death that he would die. And we saw, as sure as the earth beneath our feet, that to stay with him would be to share that death, and that is why we left—giving only our gifts, withholding the rest.

"And now, brothers, I will ask you a terrible question,

and God knows I ask it also of myself. Is the truth beyond all truths, beyond the stars, just this: that to live without him is the real death, that to die with him is the only life?"

THE SHEPHERD

And in that region there were shepherds out in the field, keeping watch over their flock by night. And an angel of the Lord appeared to them, and the glory of the Lord shone around them, and they were filled with fear. And the angel said to them, "Be not afraid; for behold, I bring you good news of a great joy which will come to all the people; for to you is born this day in the city of David a Savior, who is Christ the Lord. And this will be a sign for you: you will find a babe wrapped in swaddling cloths and lying in a manger." And suddenly there was with the angel a multitude of the heavenly host praising God and saying, "Glory to God in the highest, and on earth peace among men with whom he is pleased!" When the angels went away from them into heaven, the shepherds said to one another, "Let us go over to Bethlehem and see this thing that has happened, which the Lord has made known to us." And they went with haste, and found Mary and Joseph, and the babe lying in a manger. And when they saw it they made known the saying which had been told them concerning this child; and all who heard it wondered at what the shepherds told them.

Luke 2:8–18 RSV

"NIGHT WAS COMING ON, and it was cold," the shepherd said, "and I was terribly hungry. I had finished all the bread I had in my sack, and my gut still ached for more. Then I noticed my friend, a shepherd like me, about to throw away a crust he didn't want. So I said, 'Throw the crust to me, friend!' and he did throw it to me, but it landed between us in the mud where the sheep had mucked it up. But I grabbed it anyway and stuffed it, mud and all, into my mouth. And as I was eating it, I suddenly saw—myself. It

was as if I was not only a man eating but a man watching
the man eating. And I thought, 'This is who I am. I am a
man who eats muddy bread.' And I thought, 'The bread is
very good.' And I thought, 'Ah, and the mud is very good
too.' So I opened my muddy man's mouth full of bread, and
I yelled to my friends, 'By God, it's good, brothers!' And
they thought I was a terrible fool, but they saw what I meant.
We saw everything that night, everything. Everything!

"Can I make you understand, I wonder? Have you ever
had this happen to you? You have been working hard all
day. You're dog-tired, bone-tired. So you call it quits for a
while. You slump down under a tree or against a rock or
something and just sit there in a daze for half an hour or a
million years, I don't know, and all this time your eyes are
wide open looking straight ahead someplace but they're so
tired and glassy they don't see a thing. Nothing. You could
be dead for all you notice. Then, little by little, you begin
to come to, then your eyes begin to come to, and all of a
sudden you find out you've been looking at something the
whole time except it's only now you really see it—one of the
ewe lambs maybe, with its foot caught under a rock, or the
moon scorching a hole through the clouds. It was there all
the time, and you were looking at it all the time, but you
didn't see it till just now.

"That's how it was this night, anyway. Like finally
coming to—not things coming out of nowhere that had never
been there before, but things just coming into focus that had
been there always. And such things! The air wasn't just
emptiness any more. It was alive. Brightness everywhere,
dipping and wheeling like a flock of birds. And what you
always thought was silence stopped being silent and turned
into the beating of wings, thousands and thousands of them.

Only not just wings, as you came to more, but voices—high, wild, like trumpets. The words I could never remember later, but something like what I'd yelled with my mouth full of bread. 'By God, it's good, brothers! The crust. The mud. Everything. Everything!'

"Oh well. If you think we were out of our minds, you are right, of course. And do you know, it was just like being out of jail. I can see us still. The squint-eyed one who always complained of sore feet. The little sawed-off one who could outswear a Roman. The young one who blushed like a girl. We all tore off across that muddy field like drunks at a fair, and drunk we were, crazy drunk, splashing through a sea of wings and moonlight and the silvery wool of the sheep. Was it night? Was it day? Did our feet touch the ground?

" 'Shh, shh, you'll wake up my guests,' said the Innkeeper we met coming in the other direction with his arms full of wood. And when we got to the shed out back, one of the three foreigners who were there held a finger to his lips.

"At the eye of the storm, you know, there's no wind— nothing moves—nothing breathes—even silence keeps silent. So hush now. Hush. There he is. You see him? You see him?

"By Almighty God, brothers. Open your eyes. Listen."

The End Is Life

*Next day, that is, after the day of Preparation,
the chief priests and the Pharisees gathered before Pilate and
said, "Sir, we remember how that impostor said, while he was
still alive, 'After three days I will rise again.' Therefore order
the sepulchre to be made secure until the third day, lest his disciples go and steal him away, and tell the people, 'He has risen
from the dead,' and the last fraud will be worse than the first."
Pilate said to them, "You have a guard of soldiers; go, make it as
secure as you can." So they went and made the sepulchre secure
by sealing the stone and setting a guard.* Matthew 27:62–66 RSV

TO BEGIN WITH, let us first consider the words
of the governor—the ones that he spoke to the delegation
when they confronted him with their darkest fears and suspicions and asked for his help. To be more accurate, one
should say *"almost* their darkest fears and suspicions" because
there was one even darker still, which for good reason they
left unspoken. Let us consider the words of Pontius Pilate,
that apprehensive, puzzled, somehow doomed Roman pa-
trician who had at least the virtue of great patience. Heaven
knows they had put him through plenty already: forcing
him to take official cognizance of an incident that he would
certainly have preferred to overlook; insisting that he try the
man for offenses against Jewish piety when as far as he was
concerned Jewish piety could not have mattered less; and
finally threatening to inform against him to his patron and
emperor, Tiberius Caesar, if he did not yield to their pressure
and have the man executed, which, of course, he finally did,
although not before announcing first that as far as he was

concerned the man was innocent, and then publicly washing his hands to symbolize his wish to disassociate himself personally from the whole dirty business. Let it be on the heads of the barbarians.

And then, on the day after the sentence had been carried out, when he might very reasonably have believed that at last the case could be considered closed for good, there they were back at him again—the same crowd of chief priests and Pharisees, still clamoring at him with their complaints and petitions. It is to Pilate's credit as both a Roman and a civil servant, I think, that he seems to have kept his words entirely free from any trace of irritation when with great economy he answered them by saying simply, "You have a guard of soldiers; go, make it as secure as you can." These are the words to consider.

Of all the great painters of the world, the one that I would choose to paint this scene is Rembrandt. I would want it done in chiaroscuro, in terms of light and shade, with the chamber where Pilate receives the delegation almost entirely in shadow and with the light coming mainly from the faces themselves, especially the bearded faces of the Jewish elders, the creased faces of these pious old men as they lean a little too intensely forward to hear the Roman's answer. What will he say? Then the helpless, old-man look when they are not quite sure that they have heard correctly as Pilate tells them in effect to do whatever they want to do. They have their own Temple guard, after all. "Make it as secure as you can," he tells them. This is precisely the moment for Rembrandt to paint: the venerable old men turning toward each other now, their faded old eyes wide with bewilderment, their mouths hanging loose—the kind of dazed, tremulous fear of old men suddenly called upon to do a young man's job.

You are not sure whether to laugh or to cry. "As secure as you can," the Procurator of Judea tells them. But how secure is that? Their lips move, but no sound comes. God knows they have good reason to be afraid.

God knows. I think that we can say they have two reasons for being afraid, although they mentioned only one to Pilate, namely, that the dead man's disciples may, in the words of Matthew, "go and steal him away and tell the people, 'He has risen from the dead' " in which case, they explain, "the last fraud will be worse than the first"—the first being the man's claim to have been the Messiah, the *Christos*, Christ. So their spoken fear is just that—the fear of a religious hoax. But as fears go, that is not such a terrible one really because in the not so long run religious hoaxes always tend to burn themselves out as the chief priests and the Pharisees had good reason to know, living as they did in an age when would-be Messiahs were a dime a dozen, so much so that you had a hard time remembering even their names let alone the wild rumors of miracle that circulated about them for a little while.

So, even if the disciples were successful in their theft of the body, and even if for a time their claim of resurrection flourished, it could not really flourish long without something more substantial than merely rumor to feed upon. The Jewish elders must have been perfectly aware of this, of course, yet they gave all the signs of being really very afraid anyway. In other words, beneath the fear that they spoke about to Pilate lay another fear that they had not spoken about to anyone probably, not even to each other. This was the fear which I doubt very much if any one of them had had the courage to face more than fleetingly even within the secrecy of his own heart—the fear that the man whom they had crucified would *really* come alive again as he had promised, that the body that now lay dead in its tomb, disfigured by the mutilations of the Cross, that this body or some new and terrible version of it would start to breathe again, stand up in its grave clothes and move toward them with unspeakable power. To the extent that deep within themselves the Jewish elders feared this as a real possibility, their being told by Pilate to make things as secure as they could was to have the very earth pulled out from under them. How does an old man keep the sun from rising? How do soldiers secure the world against miracle?

Yet maybe it is not as hard as they feared. I suspect that many of us could have greatly reassured them. I suspect that many of us could tell them that all in all there is a lot one can do in defense against miracle, and, unless I badly miss my guess, there are thousands upon thousands of ministers doing precisely that at any given instant—making it as secure as they can, that is, which is really quite secure indeed. The technique of the chief priests and the Pharisees was to seal the tomb with a boulder and then to post a troop of guards to keep watch over it; but even for its time that was crude. The point is not to try to prevent the thing from happening—like trying to stop the wind with a machine gun —but, every time it happens, somehow to explain it away, to deflect it, defuse it, in one way or another to dispose of it. And there are at least as many ways of doing this as there are sermons preached on Easter Sunday.

We can say that the story of the Resurrection means simply that the teachings of Jesus are immortal like the plays of Shakespeare or the music of Beethoven and that their wisdom and truth will live on forever. Or we can say that the Resurrection means that the spirit of Jesus is undying, that he himself lives on among us, the way that Socrates does, for instance, in the good that he left be-

hind him, in the lives of all who follow his great example. Or we can say that the language in which the
Gospels describe the Resurrection of Jesus is the language of
poetry and that, as such, it is not to be taken literally but as
pointing to a truth more profound than the literal. Very
often, I think, this is the way that the Bible is written, and
I would point to some of the stories about the birth of Jesus,
for instance, as examples; but in the case of the Resurrection,
this simply does not apply because there really is no story
about the Resurrection in the New Testament. Except in
the most fragmentary way, it is not described at all. There
is no poetry about it. Instead, it is simply proclaimed as a
fact. *Christ is risen!* In fact, the very existence of the New
Testament itself proclaims it. Unless something very real
indeed took place on that strange, confused morning, there
would be no New Testament, no Church, no Christianity.

Yet we try to reduce it to poetry anyway: the coming of
spring with the return of life to the dead earth, the rebirth of
hope in the despairing soul. We try to suggest that these
are the miracles that the Resurrection is all about, but they
are not. In their way they are all miracles, but they are not
this miracle, this central one to which the whole Christian
faith points.

Unlike the chief priests and the Pharisees, who tried
with soldiers and a great stone to make themselves as secure
as they could against the terrible possibility of Christ's really
rising again from the dead, we are considerably more subtle.
We tend in our age to say, "Of course, it was bound to happen. Nothing could stop it." But when we are pressed to say
what it was that actually did happen, what we are apt to
come out with is something pretty meager: this "miracle" of
truth that never dies, the "miracle" of a life so beautiful that
two thousand years have left the memory of it undimmed, the

"miracle" of doubt turning into faith, fear into hope. If I believed that this or something like this was all that the Resurrection meant, then I would turn in my certificate of ordination and take up some other profession. Or at least I hope that I would have the courage to.

If I thought that when you strip it right down to the bone, this whole religion business is really just an affirmation of the human spirit, an affirmation of moral values, an affirmation of Jesus of Nazareth as the Great Exemplar of all time and no more, then like Pilate I would wash my hands of it. The human spirit just does not impress me that much, I am afraid. And I have never been able to get very excited one way or the other about moral values. And when I have the feeling that someone is trying to set me a good example, I start edging toward the door.

So what do I believe actually happened that morning on the third day after he died? When I was young, I would never have dreamed of asking a minister that question, not even if someone had offered to pay me; and I would have to know one quite well to ask now. Nobody has ever asked it of me, and I have been asked just about everything else. I do not mean some theological version of the question: what is the relevance of the Resurrection to the doctrine of man or something. I mean the very straightforward, naked, somehow unmentionable thing itself: what do we think really happened? If you had been there yourself, what do you think you would really have seen?

One night I stood on the bridge of a small British freighter somewhere near the middle of the Atlantic. I was talking to a young junior officer with red hair who told me something that it is very useful to know. He had been looking around to see if he could spot the lights of any other ships on the horizon, and what he told me was this: the way to see lights on the horizon is not to look *at* the horizon but to look at the sky just above it. And I discovered that he was right. This is the way to do it. Since then I have learned that it is also the way to see other things.

I do not think that I would have looked straight at the tomb if I had been there, at the large boulder that they had rolled up to seal it with. I do not think that I could have even if I had wanted to, in that queer, seething light between night and daybreak when you cannot look long at anything before it begins to disappear. I would have looked just above it, or off to one side.

One of the guardsmen asleep on the ground, his helmet resting in the crook of one arm, his other arm flung out on the damp grass. He stirs in his sleep and murmurs something unintelligible. Then, lying there on his back in the dark, he suddenly opens his eyes: the fire of a billion stars.

Or the leaves of an olive tree, gray-green, unmoving in the still air. Nothing moves. Then, out of nowhere, a breeze comes up—stiff and fresh and smelling of the dawn: underneath, each olive leaf is the color of silver.

A voice is shouting, high and soft and from far away like the voice a child hears calling him home, at the end of a long summer dusk. The sound of running feet.

I cannot tell you anything more than this about what I think I would have seen if I had been there myself. No man can honestly. I do not believe that even the ones who actually were there could have told you more, if any were there and had stayed awake.

But I can tell you this: that what I believe happened and what in faith and with great joy I proclaim to you here is that he somehow *got up*, with life in him again, and the glory upon him. And I speak very plainly here, very unfancifully, even though I do not understand well my own lan-

guage. I was not there to see it any more than I was awake
to see the sun rise this morning, but I affirm it as surely as
I do that by God's grace the sun did rise this morning because that is why the world is flooded with light.

He got up. He said, "Don't be afraid." Rich man, poor
man, child; sick man, dying; man who cannot believe, scared
sick man, lost one. Young man with your life ahead of you.
"Don't be afraid."

He said, "Feed my sheep," which is why, like the chief
priests and the Pharisees, we try to make that tomb as secure
as we can. Because this is what he always says: "Feed my
sheep . . . my lambs." And this is what we would make ourselves secure from, knowing the terrible needs of the lambs
and our abundance, knowing our own terrible needs.

He said, "Lo, I am with you always, even unto the end
of the world."

Anxiety and fear are what we know best in this fantastic
century of ours. Wars and rumors of wars. From civilization
itself to what seemed the most unalterable values of the past,
everything is threatened or already in ruins. We have heard
so much tragic news that when the news is good we cannot
hear it.

But the proclamation of Easter Day is that all is well. And
as a Christian, I say this not with the easy optimism of one
who has never known a time when all was not well but as
one who has faced the Cross in all its obscenity as well as in
all its glory, who has known one way or another what it is
like to live separated from God. In the end, his will, not
ours, is done. Love is the victor. Death is not the end. The
end is life. His life and our lives through him, in him. Existence has greater depths of beauty, mystery, and benediction
than the wildest visionary has ever dared to dream. Christ
our Lord has risen.

The Road to Emmaus

That very day two of them were going to a village named Emmaus, about seven miles from Jerusalem, and talking with each other about all these things that had happened. While they were walking and discussing together, Jesus himself drew near and went with them. But their eyes were kept from recognizing him. And he said to them, "What is this conversation which you are holding with each other as you walk?" And they stood still, looking sad. Then one of them, named Cleopas, answered him, "Are you the only visitor to Jerusalem who does not know the things that have happened there in these days?" And he said to them, "What things?" And they said to him, "Concerning Jesus of Nazareth, who was a prophet mighty in deed and word before God and all the people, and how our chief priests and rulers delivered him up to be condemned to death, and crucified him. But we had hoped that he was the one to redeem Israel. Yes, and besides all this, it is now the third day since this happened. Moreover, some women of our company amazed us. They were at the tomb early in the morning and did not find his body; and they came back saying that they had even seen a vision of angels, who said that he was alive. Some of those who were with us went to the tomb, and found it just as the women had said; but him they did not see." And he said to them, "O foolish men, and slow of heart to believe all that the prophets have spoken! Was it not necessary that the Christ should suffer these things and enter into his glory?" And beginning with Moses and all the prophets, he interpreted to them in all the scriptures the things concerning himself.

So they drew near to the village to which they were going. He appeared to be going further, but they constrained him, saying, "Stay with us, for it is toward evening and the day is now far spent." So he went in to stay with them. When he was at

table with them, he took the bread and blessed, and broke it, and
gave it to them. And their eyes were opened and they recognized
him; and he vanished out of their sight. They said to each other,
"Did not our hearts burn within us while he talked to us on the
road, while he opened to us the scriptures?" And they rose that
same hour and returned to Jerusalem; and they found the eleven
gathered together and those who were with them, who said, "The
Lord has risen indeed, and has appeared to Simon!" Then they
told what had happened on the road, and how he was known to
them in the breaking of the bread.   Luke 24:13–35 RSV

LATE FRIDAY AFTERNOON HE DIED, and then
there was Saturday, which should have been the worst day
except that somehow or other perhaps it was not. If for even
as much as an instant we look up into the full brilliance of
the sun, we find that for hours afterward whenever we close
our eyes the outline of the sun is still there as though the
image had been branded on our eyelids; and so it must have
been for the ones who had been present that Friday on the
hill where he was executed. On Saturday, the Jewish Sabbath,
even with their eyes closed, they could still see the three
crosses dark and angular against the sky; even with their
fingers in their ears, they could still hear the sounds that had
been made up there: the cry of thirst, the buzzing of the
flies, and the heat, because heat has a sound too, like a
muffled drum or the beating of a heart. But the poet was
right who said that "After great pain a formal feeling comes,"
and for the people who had loved the man and had gone up
Friday to be near him when he died, Saturday must have
been a strangely formal day too, the way the day after the
death of someone we love is always a formal day: when we
arrange our faces carefully and our words carefully, and we
are even careful where we put our feet because we have the

feeling that one careless step and earth and heaven both
might split in two about us. The way if somebody in our
family dies, when we go back after the funeral, things are
quite different for a while: people are very polite and a little
stiff with us, and are apt to straighten their ties and start
talking about the weather when we enter the room. But the
world of course never lets us be formal for long. All of a
sudden, before we know it, it is back to its old tricks again:
pulling the chair out from under us just as we are about to
sit down; just as the lumps in our throats are about to burst,
blowing trumpets in our ears or setting off firecrackers. And
perhaps that is the worst time of all—when we realize that
life is going to have to go on the same way it always has except
that of course it will never be the same again.

So for at least some of the followers of Jesus, maybe the
worst day was the third one, Sunday, which for the Jews was
like our Monday, with everything around them returning so
completely to normal that it was impossible to believe that
either his life or his death was going to make any difference
to the world at all. When they were suddenly afraid that the
whole business of his life had not really added up to much.
He had made great promises and great claims, and a number
of people had placed all their greatest hopes in him. But now
he was dead. Of course there were rumors about the tomb's
being empty. The women had come back just after sunrise
full of wild stories. But rumors are only rumors, women are
always telling wild stories, and for at least two of the people
who had followed him, there was nothing left to do that
Sunday but get out of town. And where did they go? They
went to Emmaus. And where was Emmaus and why did
they go there? It was no place in particular really, and the
only reason that they went there was that it was some seven

miles distant from a situation that had become unbearable.

Do you understand what I mean when I say that there is not one of us who has not gone to Emmaus with them? Emmaus can be a trip to the movies just for the sake of seeing a movie or to a cocktail party just for the sake of the cocktails. Emmaus may be buying a new suit or a new car or smoking more cigarettes than you really want, or reading a second-rate novel or even writing one. Emmaus may be going to church on Sunday. Emmaus is whatever we do or wherever we go to make ourselves forget that the world holds nothing sacred: that even the wisest and bravest and loveliest decay and die; that even the noblest ideas that men have had—ideas about love and freedom and justice—have always in time been twisted out of shape by selfish men for selfish ends. Emmaus is where we go, where these two went, to try to forget about Jesus and the great failure of his life.

It is a strange story. All the stories about how Jesus appeared to people after his death are strange, and the strangest thing about them is how unglamorous they are, how little fanfare there is about them. If you or I had written them, it would have been hard to resist giving them a little more drama. In the stories about how he was born, there is a whole choir of angels singing "Glory to God in the highest" and kings arriving from the East with precious gifts; the shepherds coming in out of the night to kneel at the manger; and the star. But here, for instance, all we have are two men walking along a dusty road to a town that nobody had heard of much, suddenly aware of footsteps approaching them from behind and being joined then by a stranger who was Jesus but whom they did not even recognize, perhaps because even when he was alive they had never really recognized him, had seen him not as he actually was but only as they had wanted

him to be: a hero who would give them a lot of easy answers
to all of life's hardest questions, questions about love and
pain and goodness and death. So they were joined by this
Jesus, whom they did not recognize, and when they reached
the village of Emmaus, and because it was getting late, they
persuaded him to stop and have supper with them. And it
was only then, only as he took the bread and blessed it and
broke it, that they knew who he was. And no sooner did
they know who he was than he vanished from their sight.
Much as they would have given to have had him stay there
a minute or two more, they could not make him stay. They
could not nail him down. And that is how it always is. We
can never nail him down, not even if the nails we use are real
ones and the thing we nail him to is a cross. He comes suddenly, out of nowhere, like the first clear light of the sun
after a thunderstorm or maybe like the thunder itself; and
maybe we recognize him, and maybe we do not, and our lives
are never the same again either because we did not recognize
him or because we did.

And the place where he comes is very apt to be Emmaus,
which is the place where we spend much of our lives, you
and I, the place that we go to in order to escape—a bar, a
movie, wherever it is we throw up our hands and say, "Let
the whole damned thing go hang. It makes no difference anyway." But there are some things that even in Emmaus we
cannot escape. We can escape our troubles, at least for a
while. We can escape the job we did not get or the friend
we hurt. We can even escape for a while the awful suspicion
that life makes no sense and that the religion of Jesus is just
a lot of wishful thinking. But the one thing that we cannot
escape is life itself: the fact that I am here on this earth, a
living human being with blood in my veins and breath in my

lungs. We cannot escape getting hungry, and we cannot escape eating. We cannot escape walking or driving down a dusty road to get from one place to another. And my point is this, that it is precisely at such times as these that life is going to ask us questions that we cannot escape for long: questions about where the road we are traveling is finally going to take us; about whether food is enough to keep us alive, truly alive; about who we are and who the stranger is behind us.

In other words, it is precisely at such times as these that Jesus is apt to come, into the very midst of life at its most real and inescapable. Not in a blaze of unearthly light, not in the midst of a sermon, not in the throes of some kind of religious daydream, but . . . at supper time, or walking along a road. This is the element that all the stories about Christ's return to life have in common: Mary waiting at the empty tomb and suddenly turning around to see somebody standing there—someone she thought at first was the gardener; all the disciples except Thomas hiding out in a locked house, and then his coming and standing in the midst; and later, when Thomas was there, his coming again and standing in the midst; Peter taking his boat back after a night at sea, and there on the shore, near a little fire of coals, a familiar figure asking, "Children, have you any fish?"; the two men at Emmaus who knew him in the breaking of the bread. He never approached from on high, but always in the midst, in the midst of people, in the midst of real life and the questions that real life asks.

The sacred moments, the moments of miracle, are often the everyday moments, the moments which, if we do not look with more than our eyes or listen with more than our ears, reveal only . . . the gardener, a stranger coming down the road behind us, a meal like any other meal. But if we look with our hearts, if we listen with all of our being and our imagination—if we live our lives not from vacation to vacation, from escape to escape, but from the miracle of one instant of our precious lives to the miracle of the next—what we may see is Jesus himself, what we may hear is the first faint sound of a voice somewhere deep within us saying that there is a purpose in this life, in our lives, whether we can understand it completely or not; and that this purpose follows behind us through all our doubting and being afraid, through all our indifference and boredom, to a moment when suddenly we know for sure that everything does make sense because everything is in the hands of God, one of whose names is forgiveness, another is love. This is what the stories about Jesus' coming back to life mean, because Jesus was the love of God, alive among us, and not all the cruelty and blindness of men could kill him.

If someone wants proof that he is alive and that this is so, all I can say in honesty is that I have none to give. No preacher can prove it, no teacher, no book, not even the Bible. It defies logic and reason, and it breaks the laws of nature as we understand them. If we are to believe he is really alive with all that that implies, then we have to believe without proof. And of course that is the only way it could be. If it could be somehow proved, then we would have no choice but to believe. We would lose our freedom not to believe. And in the very moment that we lost that freedom, we would cease to be human beings. Our love of God would have been forced upon us, and love that is forced is of course not love at all. Love must be freely given. Love must live in the freedom not to love; it must take risks. Love must be prepared to suffer even as Jesus on the Cross suffered, and part of that suffering is doubt, even as Jesus on the Cross doubted.

But if we have no proof that he is alive, we have many witnesses, two thousand years of them, and yet we have more than that. We have the witness of our own lives, or at least of certain deep moments when we were truly alive and when, if only for a minute or two, we have seen in the breaking of a piece of bread, for instance, not just a piece of bread breaking, but something broken for us, a givenness, a source of life. The tale that Christianity tells is the tale of a sinless life given away, in love, to make up in some unfathomable way for all that we mean by our sin, to give us life in place of all that we mean by death. The greatest miracle that Christianity has to proclaim is that the love that suffered agonies on that hill outside the city walls was the love of God himself, the love of God for his creation, which is a love that has no limit, not even the limit of death. And for us the meaning of that love is that we can now raise our own shrill voices from the hills of our own suffering and say some such words as these:

There is little that we can point to in our lives as deserving anything but God's wrath. Our best moments have been mostly grotesque parodies. Our best loves have been almost always blurred with selfishness and deceit. But there is something to which we can point. Not anything that we ever did or were, but something that was done for us by another. Not our own lives, but the life of one who died in our behalf and yet is still alive. This is our only glory and our only hope. And the sound that it makes is the sound of excitement and gladness and laughter that floats through the night air from a great banquet. It is what Christians mean by salvation, and we saw it first at Emmaus, through Jesus Christ our Lord.

The Tiger

He who has an ear, let him hear what the Spirit says to the churches. To him who conquers I will give some of the hidden manna, and I will give him a white stone, with a new name written on the stone which no one knows except him who receives it.   Revelation 2:17 RSV

THE GREAT HINDU SAINT of the nineteenth century, Ramakrishna, told a fable about a motherless tiger cub who was adopted by goats and brought up by them to speak their language, emulate their ways, eat their food, and in general to believe that he was a goat himself. Then one day a king tiger came along, and when all the goats scattered in fear, the young tiger was left alone to confront him, afraid and yet somehow not afraid. The king tiger asked him what he meant by his unseemly masquerade, but all that the young one could do in response was to bleat nervously and continue nibbling at the grass. So the tiger carried him to a pool where he forced him to look at their two reflections side by side and draw his own conclusions. When this failed, he offered him his first piece of raw meat. At first the young tiger recoiled from the unfamiliar taste of it, but then as he ate more and began to feel it warming his blood, the truth gradually became clear to him. Lashing his tail and digging his claws into the ground, the young beast finally raised his head high, and the jungle trembled at the sound of his exultant roar.

Despite all the profound differences between Hinduism, Buddhism, Judaism, and Islam, they agree with each other by and large and with Christianity on one very general but very basic point: that human beings as they usually exist in this world are not what they were created to be. The goat is not really a goat at all—he is really a tiger—except that he does not know that he is, with the result that for the time being he is, in a sense, really not a tiger. Or, to use another language, we were created in the image of God, but something has gone awry. Like a mirror with a crack down the middle, we give back an image that is badly distorted. Or yet again, the story of Adam is the story of each of us. We were created to serve God and each other in love, but each of us chooses instead to serve himself as God, and this means wrenching ourselves out of the kind of relationship with God and men that we were made for. Like Adam, we have all lost Paradise; and yet we carry Paradise around inside of us in the form of a longing for, almost a memory of, a blessedness that is no more, or the dream of a blessedness that may someday be again. All the great religions share this insight in one form or another, embodying it in different myths, and I believe that our own experience of ourselves confirms the truth of it. We hear much today of man's search for his own identity, and it seems to me that this is a nonreligious expression of very much the same reality. In other words, the self that each of us has to live with day in and day out under the most intimate circumstances possible is not entirely the self that we would have chosen to be tied to on such a long-term basis. Or, to return to the language of the fable, if the tiger who thinks he is a goat could really be a goat, then he would not have this problem. But fortunately, or unfortunately, there is still enough of the tiger in us to make us discontented with our goathood. We eat grass, but it never really fills us. We bleat well enough, but deep down there is the suspicion that we were really made for roaring.

One might say that the problem is how to live with a goat when the goat happens to be oneself, and all kinds of solutions have been offered. There are some, for instance, who would turn the thing on its head and say that a man's condition might be better represented by a story about a goat who has a guilt complex because he is not a tiger. In other words, accept our goathood with all its drawbacks because goats are all that we are. Adjust ourselves to the fact that the whole tiger business is just an illusion, a neurosis, and since we are goats, try at least to be well-adjusted goats. But the intuition of tigerhood remains.

There are others, and at least part of the time we are all among them, who acknowledge the problem of living with a goat when it happens to be oneself, but who advocate simply trying not to think about it. If the smell gets bad, just open the windows and let in some fresh air. When we realize that all the most succulent grass on the market will not fill the awful emptiness within us and when the sound of our own bleating begins to grate on our ears, turn on the TV sets, have another drink, try to keep busy at something. But not even the busiest schedule or the headiest drink can solve the problem permanently.

The moralistically inclined are drawn to those who maintain that it is not so bad to live with a goat if one can only housebreak him, make him into a good goat, a moral goat. But morality is apt to be just another kind of grass that fails to fill the aching void; and the man of unimpeachable conduct, the housebroken man, is apt to be more joyless, more off his true course than most.

So the problem remains. And to anyone who is looking for good reasons not to be a Christian, I can suggest none better than that to be a Christian is only to make the problem worse. Because a Christian is one who has seen the tiger. "In the juvenescence of the year," T. S. Eliot wrote, "comes Christ the Tiger," and it is a wonderful image because it cuts through so much rubbish. Not the soulful-eyed, sugar-sweet, brilliantined Christ of the terrible pictures that one can buy. But this explosion of a man, this explosion of Life itself into life.

We look at him. We glance up from our grazing for a moment, and there he stands, and suddenly we see what a tiger looks like, what a human being really looks like, and if we thought that our goathood was a problem before, our own half-baked, cockeyed humanity, we reach the point here, if we look hard, where the contrast becomes so painful that one or the other of us simply has to go. Either we crucify the tiger just to escape his terrible gaze, or we at least risk the crucifixion of our own goathood, which must go if it is to be replaced by tigerhood. In either case, our first cry when we see him is a cry of woe: if this is what it really is to be human, then what am I? If this is true life, then what is this that I am living?

People are so apt to drift along on the surface of their lives, not really seeing or hearing or feeling very much because most of the time they are little more than half alive, the rest of the time dazed, dreaming, or detached. But in Christ, as we read about him, think about him, there is this terrible quality of full life. The world always seems to be pressing in on all of him, not just on the dimension that happens to be alive at the moment. Most of us escape so much by being less than fully alive, but he seems to escape nothing: the dead sparrow, the woman touching the hem of his robe as he passes by, the disciples shooing away the children, the sawed-off little crook named Zaccheus up in a tree to see him come through town. Always, with all of himself, he seems to be vulnerable to all of it and especially to the pain that is around him, not just the pain of the crippled and the bereaved, but the slow, unspoken pain of being human. "Come unto me, all ye that labor and are heavy laden, and I will give you rest." And he means everybody because everybody labors and is heavy laden—Pilate, Judas, Albert Schweitzer, Marilyn Monroe, Adolf Eichmann.

He does not seem to have had much sense of humor, and unconsciously, I think, we cannot quite forgive him for that because for us it is one of the major virtues; but in order to laugh, it is necessary to step back from life a little, whereas he almost never steps back but keeps moving deeper and deeper into the world's pain, everyone's pain, which becomes his own, because this is the way that love moves, that is all. And he moves into the world's joy too only there seems to have been much less of that for him, only a handful of moments as the Gospels unfold—the wedding at Cana, the field full of lilies, his lying down in the stern of Peter's boat with a pillow under his head and falling asleep there until the storm comes up. We have the sense, as we watch him, that this is what man really is, that this is what human life is really all about.

Then perhaps we say, "Woe is me. This is man as I am not. This is the life I do not live, cannot live. I am a goat, and I live in a world of goats. I adjust myself to my world. I make its standards my standards, its wisdom my wisdom, its goals my goals. And my world adjusts me to itself—where it cannot break me in, it breaks me off, breaks me up. If Christ is just an example we're supposed to follow, then he is a curse because we cannot follow, not one of us, and the way of the Christian is the way of despair." But there are other things to say.

To anyone who is looking for good reasons for being a Christian, let me suggest the only really good one that I know. What does the faith mean by taking this man who was really a man, perhaps the only man, and calling him the Son of God, the Word of God, the Christ, all these metaphors so alien to our whole way of thinking? What is the reality about him other than the reality of his manhood that these metaphors are so clumsily, hopelessly, beautifully trying to convey? Just this, I believe, and it is much: that in this man there is power to turn goats into tigers, to give life to the half-alive, even to the dead; that what he asks of us when he says "Follow me" is what he also has the power to give, and this is the power of God that he has, that he is, and that is why men have called him the Christ.

In the Book of Revelation, the Spirit is depicted as speaking to goats who cannot entirely accept their goathood, and thus to many of us who sense within ourselves a nature that we have never realized, an identity that we have never found, a life that we have never quite begun to live. And he says, "to them I will give hidden manna"—a strength beyond our strength. "To them I will give a white stone with a new name written on the stone"— and this new name is the life, the self, that in our moments of truth we yearn, above all else perhaps, to find. What he gives us is ourselves. What he tells us is our names and who we really are—God's sons, brothers to one another. And he offers us food and drink to warm our blood and make us drunk with the mystery and the joy of it.

Follow Me

As Jesus passed on from there, he saw a man called Matthew sitting at the tax office; and he said to him, "Follow me." And he rose and followed him.   Matthew 9:9 RSV

HE SAW A MAN sitting at the tax office, and he said, "Follow me," and the man followed him, and it was just as simple and just as complicated as that. If we think its simplicity sounds a little improbable—if we are inclined to question whether Matthew, the man in the tax office, would have made such an overwhelming decision so instantaneously and on the basis of what looks like such meager incentive—then we are forgetting that this is the way that men almost always make their overwhelming decisions. It is the comparatively minor decisions that take all the time and fuss. Do we take our vacation in the summer or in the fall? Do we ask the Smiths, or do we ask the Browns? On ones like these, we do not go one way or another until we have taken plenty of time to weigh all the pros and cons on both sides, and then we ask our wives what they think and toss a coin a few times, and only then—with what is by now considerably less than burning conviction—we ask the Browns, let us say, but not without a number of long backward glances directed over our shoulders at the Smiths.

But on the really crucial decisions of life—Do I love her enough to marry her? Is it worth dying for? Can I give my life to this?—when it comes to decisions like these, it is not just the pro-and-con-listing part of me or the coin-tossing and advice-seeking parts that are involved. It is all of me, heart, mind, will, and when the moment comes and I find myself moving out for good and all, one way or another, there is a kind of relentless spontaneity about it, a kind of terrific sense of conviction, so that if you are Matthew in the tax office, you lay down your slide rule and your pencil, do not even finish the form that you happened to be working on at the moment, but just push back your chair and start heading for the door without even bothering to pick up your coat hanging over by the water cooler. And then you step out of there forever without once looking back over your shoulder, and start following the way you have chosen: not that way over there or that way right here, but *this* way. Of all the ten million and one ways in the world, you choose this way. Or maybe it chooses you —to put it a better way. Or you choose each other, your way and you. And if the choice is right (whatever that means exactly), you get the feeling not that you acted on blind impulse without any preparation, but that this is the moment, the crisis, that somehow your whole life has been preparing you for. "Yes, I love—this one. For that I would be willing perhaps even to die." And the voice that you heard over your shoulder as you sat there working on form 6321B was not so much the cause of your decision as the occasion for it. The bow had already been drawn tight, the arrow already set in place and aimed for Lord knows how long. The voice just made it possible to let it fly, to give it wings.

Yet all that the voice said was, "Follow me"—no fore-warning, no explanation, no attempt to persuade. Come on. This way. I will show you. These are words that do not even need a voice to make them heard. The eyes can speak them or a pair of hands. Even silence will do. But we always answer them with our feet. We get up and start following. Or we do not. Maybe we just plant our feet squarely on the ground and pretend we did not hear. Or we move them, all right, but in another direction—to the movies, to the board-of-directors meeting, to the little room where we think our most fascinating thoughts. The words themselves we almost cannot help hearing at one time or another; but in case we have not heard them recently or in case we have been more than usually successful in mistaking them for the squeak of a hinge or the flapping of a shutter or the dry rattle of a sermon, let me say them again now: Follow him.

So then what? What now—now that the words have been spoken? There is really no telling, of course. Only the feet will finally tell. But if I had to guess, I would say, "Now the questions." Not questions that really want answers (because most of the answers we know already) but questions that want to postpone as long as possible that moment when it will be up to the feet to decide. And all the questions divide up into two categories, one for each of the two words that Matthew heard: the *follow* questions and the *me* questions.

Why *should* we *follow*? Why should *we* follow? How far do we follow? Where do we follow him? How much can we take along with us? What do we get for our pains? What will it cost us?

And then, of course, the questions about the *me*, which are really all one question and can be very simply put: who is it that speaks these words? Who is this who asks us to follow? We want to know who he is before we follow him, and that is understandable enough except that the truth of the matter is that it is only by first following him that we can begin to find out who he is. You do not come first to understand a person fully and then to love him, but love comes first, and then it is out of the love that understanding is born. And I choose the analogy carefully because it is precisely love that set this whole scene in the tax office on fire; and once we see that, we see that Jesus told Matthew to follow him not just for his own sake but for the sake of Matthew, whom he loved. And it is because Matthew knew this that he did not stop to ask any questions but merely got up and followed faithfully. Faith is the word that describes the direction our feet start moving when we find that we are loved. Faith is stepping out into the unknown with nothing to guide us but a hand just beyond our grasp.

But you and I do ask questions about what following means, and even though our questions are usually not so much interested in getting an answer as they are in drowning out the terrible sound of the answer we already know, we have to try to answer them anyway.

Where will our following take us, for instance? God only knows where it will take us, and we can be sure only that it will take us not where we want to go necessarily but where we are wanted, until, by a kind of alchemy, where we are wanted becomes where we want to go. Following may take us to a certain town where at Christmastime several years ago we would have found a group of people, some of whom were our friends, telling a young Jew who had recently become a Christian that he could not be invited to the country-club dance because he was a Jew. To follow, in this case, might have meant our doing what the Episcopal priest there did do, which was to invoke the Prayer Book restriction excluding from the Lord's Table all those who are not in love and charity with their neighbor, and on that basis to exclude those people on the club's executive committee who obviously were not in love and charity with this particular neighbor, until in some way they set things right again. It so happens that this

story has a happy ending because things were set right again
—the executive committee reversed its ruling, the committee
members were accepted back into the communion of their
church, and the club no longer excludes Jews as Jews—but to
just this extent it is a misleading story because the happy
ending tends to be the exception rather than the rule. And
even as it stands, who can tell what it may have cost the priest
to take the stand he did, or what it cost the young Jewish
Christian, or, for that matter, the committee who finally ate
their deeds in public?

It is also misleading because it tends to look like a victory
of the good-guy priest over the bad-guy committeemen,
whereas actually it was not in the name of his own goodness
that the priest passed judgment but in the name of the one
he followed. To follow means to follow, not to lead. To
point not to our own superior moral character but to the
dimly seen figure out there that we are stumbling after.

In fact, to follow means to understand with awful clarity
that we have no superior moral character in the first place but
that our guilt just has a less offensive name than, say, anti-
Semitism, or that we are more adept at keeping it under cover.
And that brings up another of these questions about what it
means to follow.

What can we take along with us on this journey to we
do not know where? What we must take is the knowledge of
our own unendingly ambiguous motives. For instance, it is
not just the love of God or even of their fellow men that
takes all the young Americans of the Operation Crossroads
Africa program to Africa each summer to build schools and
hospitals at the risk of their health if not of their lives. Love
is part of it, one hopes; but as in every other human enter-
prise, there is a good deal of self in it too—the lure of adventure, of becoming known as the kind of person who does inter-

esting things, and so on—but of course most of them know this perfectly well themselves, and yet they follow along anyway because the voice that we hear over our shoulders never says, "First be sure that your motives are pure and selfless and then follow me." If it did, then we could none of us follow. So when later on the voice says, "Take up your cross and follow me," at least part of what is meant by "cross" is our realization that we are seldom any less than nine parts fake. Yet our feet can insist on answering him anyway, and on we go, step after step, mile after mile. How far? How far?

As far as the hill where the three shadows fall and the women stand weeping beside them, only weeping not because we are to be crucified with him but because we are not to be crucified, because we guess in advance that we lack the courage unto death yet go on anyway, as far as we can, and maybe our shame, our regret, is crucifixion enough.

In what manner do we go? I want to say joyously and proudly with a spring in our step and banners flying, and sometimes by God's grace this is so. But more often than not, we go dragging our feet, wishing that we had never heard the voice that now we can never entirely stop hearing, and knowing that it is never *ours* that is the power and the glory but always *his*.

And finally, who is he? All that we know is the sound of his voice and maybe the lightest touch of his hands on our shoulders. He is the one we are free to follow or not to follow, the one we begin to know fully only by following. As we follow, we become, such as we are, his church, which is to say his body—a weak thing in most ways, half-hearted and of little faith, but full of hope for all that—and the only body that he has in this world, the only hands and feet to do his work. And such is his power that even through us others may be led to follow too.

The Me in Thee

> For I received from the Lord what I also delivered to you, that the Lord Jesus on the night when he was betrayed took bread, and when he had given thanks, he broke it, and said, "This is my body which is for you. Do this in remembrance of me." In the same way also the cup, after supper, saying, "This cup is the new covenant in my blood. Do this, as often as you drink it, in remembrance of me." For as often as you eat this bread and drink the cup, you proclaim the Lord's death until he comes.   I Corinthians 11:23–26 RSV

THE PRIMARY SYMBOL for Protestant Christianity is an empty cross, a cross with no figure on it, and the meaning is clear enough. The suffering of the crucified one is over and done with. Christ the victim of the world becomes Christ the victor over the world. Christ who is conquered by human evil and death, himself conquers them both—conquers evil by forgiving it, conquers death by life. The empty cross is a symbol of victory, Christ's victory and the victory of all who hold tight to his cross.

In the Russian Orthodox tradition, the cross is also empty, but it is a different kind of cross. Instead of an upright with just one crosspiece, it has two other smaller crosspieces as well, one just slightly above the central one and the other down toward the foot. The little one above represents the sign that they nailed over his head which bore the words "Jesus of Nazareth King of the Jews" written out in Hebrew, Latin, and Greek, so that everybody would be sure to get the point—What a king! The second little crosspiece down

toward the bottom of the cross represents the block placed
beneath his feet so that he would not fall off and end his
punishment prematurely. It is placed not at right angles to
the upright like the other two but at a slant, one end lower
than the other. This is to show that when the pain got very
bad, he pressed down on one foot, hard.

So in terms of the Russian cross, the suffering of the
crucified one is never over and done with, and Christ the
victor is also Christ the victim still. He suffers still at the
hands of the world, and he also suffers wherever anyone
suffers, and he suffers for the world's sake.

We are told that when the news of Christ's death was
brought to Pilate, Pilate found it hard to believe that it had
come about in such a short time—only six hours, from nine
in the morning until three in the afternoon or thereabout.
If a man was strong, crucifixion could last for as long as two
or three days.

The writers of the Gospels give no details about the
execution, just the words, "and they crucified him." In a way
this silence is surprising although in another way I suppose
it is not. It is also perhaps surprising that in describing his
time on the Cross, they successfully resist what must have
been the temptation to put into his mouth sentiments ap-
propriate to the occasion, edifying last words, some final ex-
hortation. But the last words that are ascribed to him could
hardly be described in such a way. He says almost nothing.
And the words that he does speak come in such short bursts
that it would not have taken much breath to say them.

At about noon, half way to the end, we are told that he
called out in a loud voice, "My God, my God, why hast thou
forsaken me?" If he was to be really a man, if he was to

know in its fullness what it means to live out a human life, if he was to understand that final suffering and humiliation of which men are capable, then he had to know this: the sense of abandonment by God. Why hast thou? Why? When the evil in the world seems greater than the mind can ascribe to the world alone. *Why?* Yet the paradox of faith then. Why hast *thou?* O thou who art more near than breathing, who formed me in my mother's womb, why art thou so far off, most near one? *My* God.

And he said, "I thirst." One remembers another king of the Jews born at Bethlehem, David, who, standing among his warriors far from home, said, "O that some one would give me water to drink from the well of Bethlehem . . . ." Three of his men broke through the ranks of the Philistines to get it for him. When they returned, the King poured it out upon the ground. "Shall I drink the lifeblood of these men? For at the risk of their lives they brought it." The splendor of the King's gesture is sweeter than water both to their lips and to his own. The lips of the Nazarene move like stones, without water or any splendor.

"One of the criminals who were hanged taunted him, saying, 'Are you not the Christ? Save yourself and us!' But the other rebuked him, saying, 'Have you no fear of God? For us it is plain justice, but this man has done nothing wrong.' And he said, 'Jesus remember me when you come in your kingly power.' And Jesus said to him, 'Today you will be with me in Paradise.'"

We can imagine the soldiers smiling as simple men do when they encounter the unforeseen—these three criminals with their swollen tongues, like frogs croaking to each other of Paradise.

The love for equals is a human thing—of friend for friend, brother for brother. It is to love what is loving and lovely. The world smiles.

The love for the less fortunate is a beautiful thing—the love for those who suffer, for those who are poor, the sick, the failures, the unlovely. This is compassion, and it touches the heart of the world.

The love for the more fortunate is a rare thing—to love those who succeed where we fail, to rejoice without envy with those who rejoice, the love of the poor for the rich, of the black man for the white man. The world is always bewildered by its saints.

And then there is the love for the enemy—love for the one who does not love you but mocks, threatens, and inflicts pain. The tortured's love for the torturer. This is God's love. It conquers the world.

It is not unusual when a person dies for the people who knew him best and loved him most to try to remember the last time that they ever saw him or the last time, like Christmas for instance, or somebody's birthday, or a picnic on the beach, when they all came together, perhaps ate together, when they all *were* together in the special way that people who love each other are at some special moment like that. And then, as time goes by and Christmas comes round again, or that birthday, or another picnic on that same beach, the person who has since died is apt to be very much on the minds of the people who are there. They may never actually mention his name for fear of seeming sentimental or of upsetting the others or perhaps just from fear of upsetting themselves, but that does not greatly matter. Because the air rings loud, of course, with the name that they do not mention, and in a unique sense he is with them there, the absent one. He is there at least as a memory, at least as a lump in the throat, but maybe as much more than that. He may be there as a presence, a benediction, a terrible reproach, or possibly as all of these at once.

It is with something like this, I think, that you have to start if you try to understand why it is that in all of its long history and in most of its many branches, the Christian faith has made so much of the Last Supper. To begin with it was, of course, the *last* supper. They never all ate together again. In a sense they never even saw him again, at least not really, because within a few hours of their eating, all Hell broke loose, to put it quite literally. It was night time, and there were soldiers, and there was the fear of their own deaths as well as of his, and they were scared stiff, and so it seems unlikely that from that time forward they saw anything very clearly except their own terror or heard anything very clearly except the pounding of their own hearts. So that supper was virtually if not in fact the last time that they saw him, and they had good reason to know that it was even at the time.

Certainly he knew it, and he did not have to be omniscient to know it either. Anybody with eyes in his head could see that the Romans and the Jews alike were out to get him. He had attacked the Jews' most ancient and sacred tradition, which was their Law, and he was a threat also to what the Romans held most sacred, which was, ironically, peace in the Empire, the *pax Romana*. He had every reason to know that his death was upon him, and although it would seem that he could have avoided it easily enough—all that he had to do, presumably, was to get out of the city and lay low for a while —he chose to stay and die because he was convinced that this was the will of God. He felt that his death was necessary if the world was to be saved from the very evil that was destroying him.

He spoke of his death this way, and as he spoke, he performed a symbolic act, taking up the loaf of bread, breaking it in his hands, and saying, "This is my body which is broken for you"—in other words, "I die willingly, for your sake, just as I break this bread now for your sake." And then the cup of wine, which he spoke of as the blood that he would shed for them Afterward, he invited the disciples to eat and drink this food, and with this the symbol is expanded somewhat and shifted; that is, he invites them to share in his life, to take his life into themselves, to live out in their own lives both the suffering and also the joy of it. And for all these centuries the Church has been re-enacting this last supper as a symbol of these things, a symbol of his giving his life away for the sake of the world, and a symbol of his followers' participating in this life, this giving.

The mystery of symbols is that a symbol contains some of the power of the thing that it symbolizes. A piece of colored cloth, a flag, for instance, has the power to move men to the same kind of fervor and action that the nation itself can. Or if we hear somebody's name—which is a symbol for the person himself—it has the power to make our hearts beat faster or strike fear in our souls, which is part of the power that the person has. As for the symbols of the Last Supper, Protestants argue with Roman Catholics, and they both argue among themselves, as to precisely how the power of Christ is present in the symbols of bread and wine; but I think that it is not too great an oversimplification to say that they all agree that one way or another, extraordinary power is there. Extraordinary because they contain a power that does not simply make the heart beat faster, say, but power that can transform a human life into a new kind of life altogether—a life like his, with some of his power in it.

At the end of Ernest Hemingway's *For Whom the Bell Tolls*, the hero, Robert Jordan, is fatally wounded by the Spanish Fascists, and the girl he loves, Maria, whom he has nicknamed Rabbit, wants to stay behind and die with him, but he tells her that she must go on and live. It is a very powerful scene, and the words that Robert Jordan uses as he tells her to go suggest much, I think, about what Christ is saying to mankind.

> "Now you will go for us both," he said. "You must do your duty now. . . . Now you are going well and fast and far and we both go in thee. . . . Now art thou doing what thou should. Now thou art obeying. Not me but us both. The me in thee. Now you go for us both. Truly. We both go in thee now. This I have promised thee."
>
> She started to look around. "Don't look around," Robert Jordan said. "Go." And Pablo hit the horse across the crupper with a hobbling strap and it looked as though Maria tried to slip from the saddle but Pilar and Pablo were riding close against her and Pilar was holding her and the three horses were going up the draw.
>
> "Roberto," Maria turned and shouted. "Let me stay! Let me stay!"
>
> "I am with thee," Robert Jordan shouted. "I am with thee now. We are both there. Go!" Then they were out of sight around the corner of the draw and he was soaking wet with sweat and looking at nothing.

Again and again over the centuries the ancient drama of Holy Communion, the Eucharist, the Mass, is acted out all over Christendom. The bread is broken and eaten, the wine drunk—these symbols with all their power to move deeply, to stir up a new kind of life in the human heart. "The me in thee. This I have promised thee." It is the greatest promise of the Christian faith, and it is the holiest mystery.

Part III
THE MYSTERY AND MIRACLE OF GRACE

*And in the last days it shall be, God declares,
that I will pour out my Spirit upon all flesh. . . .*
Acts 2:17 RSV

The Breath of Life

The woman said to him, "Sir, I perceive that you are a prophet. Our fathers worshiped on this mountain; and you say that in Jerusalem is the place where men ought to worship." Jesus said to her, "Woman, believe me, the hour is coming when neither on this mountain nor in Jerusalem will you worship the Father. You worship what you do not know; we worship what we know, for salvation is from the Jews. But the hour is coming, and now is, when the true worshipers will worship the Father in spirit and truth, for such the Father seeks to worship him. God is spirit, and those who worship him must worship in spirit and truth." John 4:19-24 RSV

"I SHALL GO TO MY GRAVE," a friend of mine once wrote me, "feeling that Christian thought is a dead language—one that feeds many living ones to be sure, one that still sets these vibrating with echoes and undertones, but which I would no more use overtly than I would speak Latin." I suppose he is right, more right than wrong anyway. If the language that clothes Christianity is not dead, it is at least, for many, dying; and what is really surprising, I suppose, is that it has lasted as long as it has.

Take any English word, even the most commonplace, and try repeating it twenty times in a row—*umbrella*, let us say, *umbrella, umbrella, umbrella*—and by the time we have finished, *umbrella* will not be a word any more. It will be a noise only, an absurdity, stripped of all meaning. And when we take even the greatest and most meaningful words that the Christian faith has and repeat them over and over again for some two thousand years, much the same thing happens. There was a time when such words as *faith, sin, redemption,* and *atonement* had great depth of meaning, great reality; but through centuries of handling and mishandling they have tended to become such empty banalities that just the mention of them is apt to turn people's minds off like a switch, and wise and good men like this friend of mine whom I have quoted wonder seriously why anyone at all in tune with his times should continue using them. And sometimes I wonder myself.

But I keep on using them. I keep plugging away at the same old words. I keep on speaking the language of the Christian faith because, although the words themselves may well be mostly dead, the longer I use them, the more convinced I become that the realities that the words point to are very real and un-dead, and because I do not happen to know any other language that for me points to these realities so well. Certain branches of psychology point to them, certain kinds of poetry and music, some of the scriptures of Buddhism and other religions. But for me, threadbare and exhausted as the Christian language often is, it remains the richest one even so. And when I ask myself, as I often do, what it is that I really hope to accomplish as a teacher of "religion," I sometimes think that I would gladly settle for just the very limited business of clarifying to some slight degree the meaning of four or five of these great, worn-out Christian words, trying to suggest something of the nature of the experiences that I believe they are describing. One of them occurs in this conversation between Jesus and the woman at the well, and it is the word "spirit"—the spirit of God that hovered like a bird over the dark waters of chaos in the first chapter of Genesis, spirit in the sense that Jesus uses it when he says that God is spirit.

When ancient man confronted the mystery of death, which is also the mystery of life—when he looked at the body of a dead man and compared it with himself as a living man and wondered at what terrible change had come over it—one of the first things that struck him apparently was that whereas he himself, the living man, breathed, the dead man did not breathe. There was no movement of the chest. A feather held to his lips remained unstirred. So to be dead meant to have no breath, and to be alive—to have the power to rise up and run and shout in the world—meant to have breath. And the conclusion, of course, was that breath is not just the little wisps of air that men breathe in and out, but that it is the very animating power of life itself. Breath is the livingness of those who are alive. This is why in so many languages the word for breath comes to mean not only the air that fills the lungs but the mystery and power of life itself that fills a living man. Such is the Latin word *spiritus*, from which our word "spirit" comes.

Each one of us has a spirit, this power of life in us, and like breath it is not just something that is in us but something that also issues from us. Every man has the capacity, more at some times than at others, to project some of this power of his own life, his vitality, into others. It is the power literally to in-spire, breathe into, and although it is invisible and intangible and cannot be put into a test tube or under a microscope, it is perhaps the greatest and most dangerous power that we have.

Team spirit, group spirit, *esprit de corps* in French—all these point to the power that can be generated by a group of people and can be generated with such force that to be in the group or even just near it is to risk being caught up by it and for a time at least transformed by it, made drunk on it. The least likely person can be so galvanized by the spirit generated by the crowd at a horse race or a football game that their madness becomes his own and he finds himself one of them. Or the least likely person can be so possessed by the spirit of a mob bent on destruction that he joins in deeds of violence and hate that otherwise he would never be capable of and that leave him, once the spirit has passed, gutted and empty like a house that has been swept by flame.

Individuals no less than groups have this power of the spirit. We can all remember certain people who were not necessarily any more intelligent or more eloquent than other people but who had this power to communicate something of their aliveness in such a way that it is part of our aliveness still. This does not come through what they say or through what they do necessarily but through what at their best they manage to be. The word "inspiring" has been so loosely used for so long that it no longer conveys very much, but again, in the literal sense, that is what such people are—life-breathing, not through deeds or words so much as through some invisible force that leaps from their lives to our lives like electricity. There are times when this force of a person is so intense that we can feel it when he just walks into a room. There is the intensity of spirit that comes with great gladness or great grief, for instance, which can gladden or grieve an entire house although the person himself may say and do nothing. It is a force that can be either creative or destructive. There are good spirits and evil spirits, and that is what makes it potentially so dangerous. In some measure everyone has the power to transform for good or ill the whole life of the community, invisibly, intangibly, but nonetheless really. And one of the strangest aspects of spirit is that it does not appear to be bound by either time or space. The spirit of a community is the product not only of all who are part of it now but of all who were part of it years ago and whose very names may no longer be remembered. By the power of your spirit, your life can reach out and become part of my life, you can empower me to do things and be things that I could never manage on my own, and this can remain true whether we are six feet apart or six thousand miles, six years or sixty. The spirit of men who died centuries ago can intoxicate us, electrify us, transform us, as really now as when they were alive.

"God" is a word three letters long, a monosyllable, a sound that the mouth makes, a mark that a pen can scratch out on paper. Written backward, it spells "dog." As a word, it is mostly dead in the sense that over the centuries it has been so drained of content that its most common use nowadays is as a mild oath. As a word it seems to point to nothing more real than a rather vague idea held more or less in common by a diminishing number of religiously inclined people. But biblically speaking, needless to say, the word "God" points not to an idea at all, and nothing could be less vague, because biblically speaking, just as you and I have a spirit, the power of life to stir life in others, so does God also have a spirit. As Jesus says in his conversation at the well, God *is* spirit. "God" is a word that describes the power deep within or beneath—whatever spatial image you like—life itself, including our lives, the spirit that enlivens our spirits.

Most of the time we tend to think of life as a neutral kind of thing, I suppose. We are born into it one fine day, given life, and in itself life is neither good nor bad except as we make it so by the way that we live it. We may make a full life for ourselves or an empty life, but no matter what we make of it, the common view is that life itself, whatever life is, does not care one way or another any more than the ocean cares whether we swim in it or drown in it. In honesty one has to admit that a great deal of the evidence supports such a view. But rightly or wrongly, the Christian faith flatly contradicts it. To say that God is spirit is to say that life does care, that the life-giving power that life itself comes from is not indifferent as to whether we sink or swim. It wants us to swim. It is to say that whether you call this life-giving power the Spirit of God or Reality or the Life Force or anything else, its most basic characteristic is that it wishes us well and is at work toward that end.

Heaven knows terrible things happen to people in this world. The good die young, and the wicked prosper, and in any one town, anywhere, there is grief enough to freeze the blood. But from deep within whatever the hidden spring is that life wells up from, there wells up into our lives, even at their darkest and maybe especially then, a power to heal, to breathe new life into us. And in this regard, I think, every man is a mystic because every man at one time or another experiences in the thick of his joy or his pain the power out of the depths of his life to bless him. I do not believe that it matters greatly what name you call this power—the Spirit of God is only one of its names—but what I think does matter, vastly, is that we open ourselves to receive it; that we address it and let ourselves be addressed by it; that we move in the direction that it seeks to move us, the direction of fuller communion with itself and with one another. Indeed, I believe that for our sakes this Spirit beneath our spirits will makes Christs of us before we are done, or, for our sakes, it will destroy us.

To Be a Saint

Another parable he put before them, saying, "The kingdom of heaven is like a grain of mustard seed which a man took and sowed in his field; it is the smallest of all seeds, but when it has grown it is the greatest of shrubs and becomes a tree, so that the birds of the air come and make nests in its branches.

Matthew 13:31–32 RSV

The kingdom of heaven is like treasure hidden in a field, which a man found and covered up; then in his joy he goes and sells all that he has and buys that field. Again, the kingdom of heaven is like a merchant in search of fine pearls, who, on finding one pearl of great value, went and sold all that he had and bought it.

Matthew 13:44–46 RSV

MY FAMILY AND I spend our summers in a house near the top of a small mountain in Vermont. We were sitting out on the terrace there one late afternoon with a couple who had come to spend the week end with us, when at a certain point the wife looked out at the hills turning lavender the way they are apt to toward evening, and at the old horses swishing their tails around to keep off the flies, and then without warning said, "There's just one thing I don't understand. Why on earth do you ever leave this place?"

I wish that I could report some stirring and edifying answer that I made: how as a minister I felt an obligation to go back to the people that I was called to minister to; how there is enough of the puritan in all of us to make us feel a little guilty about living a life that is too easy and peaceful, especially in a world where there is little ease and little peace. I might have answered too that although we love it there on the mountain, where the telephone hardly ever rings, we love it at home too, even though there the telephone hardly ever stops ringing. But as I remember, I did not answer the woman's question at all. I just made some kind of polite, vague noise; all the answers above are ones that I have thought of since. And they are all more or less true. But the question continues to outweigh all my answers put together. "Why on earth do you ever leave?" It keeps on banging in my head like a drum. I want to turn it around and ask it of the world.

Life is movement, Heaven knows. We cannot say anything about it that is surer than that. We keep leaving one kind of time for another kind of time, one place for another place, one job, one world, one set of friends, for the next, and then on to the next after that, and so on until we finally come to the end of our time and the last of our places. Whether the things that we leave are pleasant or unpleasant, peaceful or unpeaceful, we never stop leaving them for other things. That is what life is. And the innocent question that the woman asked is in a way as searching a question as it is possible to ask. Not all our "becauses" ever quite seem to drown out the great, persistent "why?" Why have we all of us left to come to wherever we are?

I have never been a great admirer of the Latin mottoes that academic institutions are apt to adorn themselves with, but the school where I serve uses one that has always struck me: *Huc venite, pueri, ut viri sitis*, or, to translate it literally, "Come to this place, little boys, in order to become men." Then, because preachers are always meddling with texts, I would like to meddle with this one to the extent of making it read, "Come to this place, all of you—come to whatever place you choose—in order to become human beings." Whether we think of it that way or not, whether we would use that kind of language to say it or not, I think that this is the deep and often unconscious motive behind all our comings and goings, behind all the scurrying around of our lives. "Why on earth do you ever leave this place?" the woman asked, while the horses stood there in the dusk swishing their tails, and if I had had my wits about me, I might have said, "I leave it in hopes of becoming a human being." No matter what a school may have to offer in the way of an education and good friends and the chance of a good job later, if it is not somehow also a place where student and teacher alike can become more and more of what it means to be truly human, then it is the wrong place for them both because without this all the rest is only busyness. If the church is not a place where we not only learn something about what it means to be human but also a place where seeds of a fuller humanity are planted in us and watered, to grow, then all our hymns and prayers and preachments are vanity.

What does it mean to be a human being? There are two fine novels, written in the last twenty-five years, one by a Roman Catholic, the other by an atheist, both of which are much involved with this question. In *The Power and the Glory*, by Graham Greene, the hero, or nonhero, is a seedy, alcoholic Catholic priest who after months as a fugitive is finally caught by the revolutionary Mexican government and condemned to be shot. On the evening before his execution, he sits in his cell with a flask of brandy to keep his courage up and thinks back over what seems to him the dingy failure of his life. "Tears poured down his face," Greene writes. "He was not at the moment afraid of damnation—even the fear of pain was in the background. He felt only an immense disappointment because he had to go to God empty-handed, with nothing done at all. It seemed to him at that moment that it would have been quite easy to have been a saint. It would only have needed a little self-restraint, and a little courage. He felt like someone who has missed happiness by seconds at an appointed place. He knew now that at the end there was only one thing that counted—to be a saint." And in the other novel, *The Plague*, by Albert Camus, there is a scrap of conversation that takes place between two atheists, one of them a journalist and the other a doctor who has been trying somehow to check the plague that has been devastating the North African city where they live. "It comes to this," says one of them. "What interests me is learning to become a saint."

Why do you ever leave this place? Why do any of us ever leave all the places and times and worlds that we are always leaving? What is the ultimate motive that underlies the unending movement of our lives? To become men, the Latin motto says, which is to become human beings. To become saints, says this odd pair of novelists, and although their word for it is different from the other, the reality that it points to is the same. To be a saint *is* to be human because we were created to be human. To be a saint is to live with courage and self-restraint, as the alcoholic priest says, but it is more than that. To be a saint is to live not with the hands clenched to grasp, to strike, to hold tight to a life that is always slipping away the more tightly we hold it; but it is to live with the hands stretched out both to give and to receive with gladness. To be a saint is to work and weep for the broken and suffering of the world, but it is also to be strangely light of heart in the knowledge that there is something greater than the world that mends and renews. Maybe more than anything else, to be a saint is to know joy. Not happiness that comes and goes with the moments that occasion it, but joy that is always there like an underground spring no matter how dark and terrible the night. To be a saint is to be a little out of one's mind, which is a very good thing to be a little out of from time to time. It is to live a life that is always giving itself away and yet is always full. The woman who asked me the question would have been justly horrified if I had answered her by saying, "I leave here to become a saint," and I would never have had the courage to say it even if it had occurred to me at the time, but in a way I believe that it is the truth for us all. Beneath all our yearning for whatever glitters brightest in this world lies our yearning for this kind of life.

The question is of course how do we find this life, how do we get to where we can live it and live it not laboriously and self-consciously because there would be no joy in that, but live it naturally and spontaneously the way the grass grows. I wish we were given a blueprint, but we are not. How do we become human beings, saints? How do we find the kingdom of Heaven? Whether we know it and acknowledge it or not, we are all voyagers on the same sea, and I suspect that the stories that describe our voyages best are ones like *Moby Dick, Huckleberry Finn, Don Quixote,* and the *Odyssey,* or any of the fairy tales that show a man starting out on a high adventure, not always sure what his goal is or what grim hazards he will meet on the way to it but sure only that the prize at the end of the road will be worth more than whatever it costs him to reach it. We are Captain Ahab out to find the great white whale, and Huck floating down the Mississippi on his raft toward freedom. We are

Odysseus lashed to the mast as the sirens sing their song, and we are Frodo the Hobbit, in Tolkien's *The Lord of the Rings,* daring all the horrors of Mordor to get rid of his terrible burden.

Jesus himself tells stories like these. There is the merchant who spends his life searching for fine pearls until finally he comes across one of such splendor that he sells all the rest to buy it. There is the man who is walking through a field somewhere when to his amazement he discovers a great treasure buried there and then "in his joy," Jesus says, sells all that he has to buy that field. Almost always when Jesus speaks of the kingdom of Heaven, there is this note of joy running through his words and with it this note of surprise: it is so much more wonderful than anyone could have dared hope, so much more within reach than anyone could have dreamed. And there is the sense too that once we have glimpsed this kingdom, tasted this life, we understand that nothing else matters—that all other pearls, next to this one, were only pearls, that every field we ever walked before was only weariness. There is only one thing that really counts, the alcoholic priest says to himself; there is only one thing that really interests him, Camus' atheist says to his companion: to be a saint, to be fully human, to enter the kingdom of Heaven, as Jesus calls it.

It is a strange and unexpected idea that this is our real business in this world, and stranger still is the idea that even if the whole subject of religion leaves us cold, as well it might, even if the very word "saint" makes our gorges rise, it is nonetheless saints that of all things we most want to become. It is joy that we are really after. God knows we settle for less —money, power, a good job, the contentment of living near the top of a small Vermont mountain—but all these things are only pearls, not ever quite the pearl that the heart longs for. It is hard to know how to find it exactly. A little more courage and self-restraint maybe. More than that. Maybe it is found best by not looking too hard for it. But this, I think, it is possible to know: that however inanely and blindly we are seeking the kingdom of Heaven, and in the damndest places, literally, it is also seeking us. Because if it is our secret purpose to become saints, it is God's unsecret purpose to make us saints. It is a "Buddha-making universe," the Buddhist scriptures proclaim, which is to say that it is the nature of reality itself to enlighten and set free the whole creation down to the last blade of grass. In Christian language, it is the ultimate purpose of God to make us all men "to the measure of the stature of the fullness of Christ."

Why on earth do we ever leave this place no matter how fair the place may be, and then the next place, and the one after that, all our lives long, and I suspect beyond our lives here, because the voyage feels as though it reaches beyond the stars? Of course we never really know. To live is to leave, that is all. But he knows. He plants the mustard seed, no bigger than the head of a pin at first. It may come with just a face that we see in a crowd, a glimpse of dawn through the window of a train, a dream that once we wake up we can never quite remember or quite forget. God's world is ablaze with miracle, and God only knows how in each of us the seed will be planted. And then, for each of us, there is a lifetime to let it grow, or fight its growing—to grow as humans, as saints, as Christs, or to kill the new life that struggles in us to be born.

A few summers ago I went on that famous March on Washington, and the clearest memory that I have of it is standing near the Lincoln Memorial hearing the song "We

Shall Overcome" sung by the quarter of a million or so people who were there. And while I listened, my eye fell on one very old Negro man, with a face like shoe leather and a sleazy suit and an expression that was more befuddled than anything else; and I wondered to myself if, quite apart from the whole civil-rights question, that poor old bird could ever conceivably overcome anything. He was there to become a human being. Well, and so were the rest of us. And so are we all, no less befuddled than he when you come right down to it. Poor old bird, poor young birds, every one of us. And deep in my heart I do believe we shall overcome some day, as he will, by God's grace, by helping the seed of the kingdom grow in ourselves and in each other until finally in all of us it becomes a tree where the birds of the air can come and make their nests in our branches. That is all that matters really.

The Breaking of Silence

And he said to them, "Which of you who has a friend will go to him at midnight and say to him, 'Friend, lend me three loaves; for a friend of mine has arrived on a journey, and I have nothing to set before him'; and he will answer from within, 'Do not bother me; the door is now shut, and my children are with me in bed; I cannot get up and give you anything'? I tell you, though he will not get up and give him anything because he is his friend, yet because of his importunity he will rise and give him whatever he needs. And I tell you, Ask, and it will be given you; seek, and you will find; knock, and it will be opened to you. For every one who asks receives, and he who seeks finds, and to him who knocks it will be opened. What father among you, if his son asks for a fish, will instead of a fish give him a serpent; or if he asks for an egg, will give him a scorpion? If you then, who are evil, know how to give good gifts to your children, how much more will the heavenly Father give the Holy Spirit to those who ask him?" Luke 11:5–13 RSV

I THINK OF THE WAITING ROOM of a railroad station late at night, or a large gallery in a museum just before closing time, or the corridor of a hospital after the patients are all asleep—some neutral, public kind of place where the light is dim and where there is an air of great stillness, isolation, a vague sense of expectancy. The place is empty except for two people, and they are standing or sitting some distance apart waiting for something, passing the time, in that strange, suspended state where time seems almost to stop because nothing is happening to mark its passage. Let us say that one of the people is you, and the other is a stranger. The silence between you is very deep, so deep that you can almost hear it, but there is no convention that says you must speak to a stranger in a public place, so it is not an embarrassing silence like the silence on occasions where human beings are expected to speak. In fact the truth of it is that for you the stranger is hardly a human being; he is a face dimly seen, a dark shape sitting on a bench or leaning against the wall. The silence, the emptiness, the preoccupation with your own thoughts and your own waiting, separate you from him as fully as light-years of space separate stars. The mystery of who you are—your loves and fears and dreams—are as hidden from him as the mystery of who he is, is hidden from you; and if somebody asked you later if there was anyone else there with you, you might say, "No. At least I don't think so. I'm not sure."

Then maybe, on impulse, you speak—"Hi . . . It's a long wait. . . ." Some silly word. Something. A very small miracle. What made you speak? God knows. Maybe a sudden pang of loneliness. A sudden desire to be known, to know. Maybe you need the sound of your own voice to bring you back to reality again from the shadow world of your introspection. But whatever the reason, you do speak; for some combination of reasons, you have to break the silence. To a stranger you reveal some part of the mystery of who you are: not just the silly words that you speak but the sense of some kind of human need that breathes behind your words. In some partial, tentative way, you open yourself to the stranger's knowing. Does he hear you? Does he answer you? If he does, a little bridge is built, and you can meet on the bridge. But does he? Is there really a person there at all, or is it just a trick of shadows?

This is what I think, in essence, prayer is. It is the

breaking of silence. It is the need to be known and the need to know. Prayer is the sound made by our deepest aloneness. I am thinking not just of formal prayers that a religious person might say in church or in bed at night, but of the kind of vestigial, broken fragments of prayer that people use without thinking of them as prayers: something terrible happens, and you might say, "God help us" or "Jesus Christ"—the poor, crippled prayers that are hidden in the minor blasphemies of people for whom in every sense God is dead except that they still have to speak to him if only through clenched teeth. Prayer is a man's impulse to open up his life at its deepest level. People pray because they cannot help it. In one way or another, I think, all people pray.

And God, of course, is the stranger. Does he listen? Does he answer? Does he exist at all? The light is so dim, and we are so caught up in ourselves, that sometimes it is hard to be sure whether the stranger is really there or just the shadow cast by our own starved longing for him.

In Luke, Jesus tells a strange story. At midnight an unexpected guest arrives. He is hungry, but you have nothing to feed him. So you go to the house of a friend to borrow some food. "Don't bother me," the friend says. "The door's locked. The children are all asleep. I can't give you anything now. Go home." But you keep on pestering him. You are so persistent that he finally gets up and gives you what you want. Then Jesus adds, "For every one who asks, receives; and he who seeks, finds; and to him who knocks, it will be opened." And his point seems to be that the secret of prayer is persistence. Keep at it, keep speaking into the darkness, and even if nothing comes, speak again and then again. And finally the answer is given.

It may not be the kind of answer that we want—the

kind of stopgap peace, the kind of easy security, the kind of
end to loneliness that we are apt to pray for. Christ never
promises peace in the sense of no more struggle and suffering.
Instead, he helps us to struggle and suffer as he did, in love,
for one another. Christ does not give us security in the sense
of something in this world, some cause, some principle, some
value, which is forever. Instead, he tells us that there is nothing in this world that is forever, all flesh is grass. He does
not promise us unlonely lives. His own life speaks loud of
how, in a world where there is little love, love is always lonely.
Instead of all these, the answer that he gives, I think, is himself. If we go to him for anything else, he may send us away
empty or he may not. But if we go to him for himself, I
believe that we go away always with this deepest of all our
hungers filled.

The shadows become a face, a presence. The stranger
turns out to be no stranger. It is not that God has to be
pestered into compassion by our persistence, but that it is
only through persistence, through hoping against hope, believing despite doubt, that a man can open himself to receive
the compassion that is there in abundance. It is only when
you ask a question out of your very bowels that the answer
is really an answer. It is only when you stretch out your hands
for it until your arms ache that a gift is really a gift.

In a way, every prayer is a prayer for healing, for your
own healing or for the healing of someone else. Healing of
the flesh or of the soul, which are so inextricably related that
to touch one is always to affect the other. You say, "God
forgive me my sin," which means, "I am empty and alone
because that is what I have done with my life and also because that is what my life has done with me. Fill the emptiness. Deliver me." You say, "Praise the Lord, O my soul,"

which means, "I am drunk with the terrible splendor of this life, but the joy is not full until I speak of it to you." You say, "The body of my friend, my child, myself, is sick. Make it well, Lord." You say, "The nations of the world snarl like wolves hungry for each other's blood. Grant them peace, Lord." The faith, such as it is, of a person when he prays, is faith in God as power. Most of the time the word "God," if it means anything, means some kind of vague idea, an oblong blur as somebody has said. But you cannot pray to an idea. When you pray, it is to a God who with at least part of yourself you believe has the power to heal, *is* the power to heal, which is the power of love.

You do not have to persuade him to heal. You do not have to ask him to change his mind and he merciful instead of indifferent. But what you do in effect, I think, is something like this. You ask God to use your prayer as a channel through which the healing power of his love can flow into whatever body or soul you pray for, your own or that of another. The channel of your praying is apt to be clogged with all kinds of doubt, not only about God but about yourself, and clogged also with disuse—and at the same time the love that you feel for the person you are praying for or for yourself is clogged with ambiguity. And yet I believe that little by little, as you persist in prayer, the power begins to trickle through anyway. The healing begins. Perhaps first it is the healing of yourself, and then gradually, through your prayer, it becomes the healing of others.

Nobody ever promised that prayer was going to be easy as far as I know, least of all anyone who ever tried it. Jesus said, "The spirit is willing, but the flesh is weak," and that meant his own flesh, too, apparently. As death drew near while he waited in the garden among shadows, he managed to choke out the words, "Not what I will, but what thou wilt," but one of the accounts says that as he did so "his sweat became like great drops of blood falling down upon the ground," and that is not hard to believe. He spoke to the stranger who is no stranger, and the answer he received was that in order to be made whole, he had first to be broken.

The disciples, in their wisdom, kept silent and addressed no word at all to the stranger for fear that he might answer them in the same way. So while Jesus prayed in the garden, they pretended to fall asleep. Or maybe they really slept. There are times when we all thirst for oblivion, and no one can blame us.

I am afraid that prayer is really not for the wise. The wise avoid it on two bases, at least two. In the first place, if there really is a God who has this power to heal, to make whole, then it is wise to be very cautious indeed because if you go to him for healing, healing may be exactly what you will receive, and are you entirely sure that you want to be healed? By all accounts, after all, the process is not necessarily either quick or easy. And in the meanwhile, things could be a great deal worse. "Lord, take my sin from me—but not yet," Saint Augustine is said to have prayed. It is a wise man who bewares of God bearing gifts. In the second place, the wise look at twentieth-century man—civilized, rational, and at great cost emancipated from the dark superstitions of the past—and suggest that to petition some unseen power for special favors is a very childish procedure indeed.

In a way, "childish" is the very word to describe it. A child has not made up his mind yet about what is and what is not possible. He has no fixed preconceptions about what reality is; and if someone tells him that the mossy place under the lilac bush is a magic place, he may wait until he thinks that no one is watching him, but then he will very probably crawl in under the lilac bush to see for himself. A child also knows how to accept a gift. He does not worry about losing his dignity or becoming indebted if he accepts it. His conscience does not bother him because the gift is free and he has not earned it and therefore really has no right to it. He just takes it, with joy. In fact, if it is something that he wants very much, he may even ask for it. And lastly, a child knows how to trust. It is late at night and very dark and there is the sound of sirens as his father wakes him. He does not explain anything but just takes him by the hand and gets him up, and the child is scared out of his wits and has no idea what is going on, but he takes his father's hand anyway and lets his father lead him wherever he chooses into the darkness.

In honesty you have to admit to a wise man that prayer is not for the wise, not for the prudent, not for the sophisticated. Instead it is for those who recognize that in face of their deepest needs, all their wisdom is quite helpless. It is for those who are willing to persist in doing something that is both childish and crucial.

Become like Children

At that time the disciples came to Jesus, saying,
"Who is the greatest in the kingdom of heaven?" And calling
to him a child, he put him in the midst of them, and said, "Truly,
I say to you, unless you turn and become like children, you will
never enter the kingdom of heaven. Whoever humbles himself
like this child, he is the greatest in the kingdom of heaven."

Matthew 18:1–4 RSV

WHAT MAKES THIS SAYING of Jesus a difficult
one, I think, is the beauty and the poetry of it. The beauty
of the words and, as in all great poetry, the shock it occasions
when, in answer to the question "Who is greatest?" he points
to the one who is least, a child—a shock that in part invites
us to look for a meaning but that in still greater part forbids
us to do so, suggesting that the meaning is essentially the
shock itself. And there is the same beauty and shock in the
setting as well: Jesus of Nazareth standing there with all the
sorrow and sin of the world fierce upon him, his very death
only a short way off, speaking this strange, almost frivolous
word, "Unless you turn and become like children . . . ." So,
reading it and being moved by the unsettling beauty of it,
we tend to pass quickly over it, and in one way this is proper
because there is a sense in which whatever is beautiful is best
seen on the run, out of the corner of the eye—to look at it
too long and too hard is to disfigure it. And there is still another danger in lingering too long over it, and that is that
there is perhaps no verse in the whole Bible which it is easier
or more tempting to sentimentalize.

Jesus says that in order to enter the kingdom of Heaven we must become like children, and this gives rise to the most poignant kind of awareness of how we ourselves were children once but are no longer, of the dreaming innocence we lost without ever intending to lose it, of a summery, green world where everything was possible, where in the end the evil dragon was always slain and the princess rescued from her tower—all of this replaced now by a winter world about which we feel that we know far too much, a world where again and again we see ourselves as not least among the dragons. And thus to read these words is to shed an inward tear, and although the tear itself is good and has much to teach us, we weep then to see ourselves weeping, and these are the tears of self-pity, and by them our vision is distorted and blurred instead of washed clean.

But despite all these dangers and difficulties, I think that from time to time we should stop at this verse and ponder its meaning because the word it speaks is no isolated word but one which runs through much of the New Testament and is far from absent in the Old. It is a word which speaks of what it is to be a child of God. It is a word which speaks through the story of how Sarah as an old woman laughed to learn that she was to bear a son, and through the name of that son, Isaac, which means laughter. It speaks through the story of King David dancing with joy before the ark of the Lord to the infinite distress of his wife. It rings out in the image of the lilies of the field, which neither toil nor spin, yet outshine Solomon in their glory. And Paul takes it up again when he writes to the Corinthians, "We are fools for Christ's sake." It is a word which speaks of the spontaneous and the debonair, of the candid, the foolish, the inarticulate.

We try so hard as Christians. We think such long thoughts, manipulate such long words, and both listen to and preach such long sermons. Each one of us somewhere, somehow, has known, if only for a moment or so, something of what it is to feel the shattering love of God, and once that has happened, we can never rest easy again for trying somehow to set that love forth not only in words, myriads of words, but in our lives themselves. And when, as must always happen, we sometimes give up this trying either because for a moment it seems unreal or because we are tired or bored or because we forget or choose to forget, we cannot even enjoy our moment's release for the sense of failure that chokes us. This is of course as it should be. Fruitless and destructive as so much of our trying must always be, and tormented as we are by knowing this and by beholding the shallowness and duplicity of our motives, we have scarcely any choice but to go on trying no matter what, and there is much that is beautiful and brave and true about it. Yet we must remember this other word too: "Unless you turn and become like children. . . ."

With our minds, we try to understand and judge our minds; with our selves, we try to control our selves; and in the process we are split in two. Even as we pray, pray carefully and well, from the secret places of our hearts, we tend to listen to ourselves praying. Even as we love, we tend to stand back from our loving as from a picture at a gallery the better to observe the splendor of it. But to be a child is to be all of one piece, to respond to life, to love, as totally and unthinkingly as even we, who are no longer children, can still respond to the sound of our own name if someone shouts it out suddenly.

The face that a child wears is his own face, whereas ours

are the faces that we have spent years arranging and re-arranging. A child is one who accepts even the most extravagant gifts, even the gift of love, not on the basis of believing that he deserves it and not in spite of the fact that he knows he does not, but simply because it is given. A child is fond of asking questions even as outrageous in their way as the questions that are asked in a seminary or a school—Why is the grass green? Where does the cat go when it is dead?—but unlike us, or maybe not entirely not unlike us, a child is not basically interested in getting an answer but only in being reassured by us, whom he asks, that we too see that the grass *is* green and that the cat *has* died. The greenness and the deadness he accepts without question.

"Who is the greatest in the kingdom of heaven?" The disciples asked this because they were trying hard, and Jesus showed them a child who in all probability neither knew nor much cared to know what the kingdom of Heaven was nor what such a question might mean. And then he told them to become like that child—neither knowing in the sense of understanding nor caring in the sense of being anxious.

And surely this is a hard saying. After we have given so much of our lives to the task of trying to understand, after we have been so continually anxious lest our faith wither and bear no fruit, then it is a real shock to be told that it is only by not trying to be that we become, that it is only by not resisting evil that we defeat it, that it is only by losing our lives that we save them. Yet if on the one hand we are shocked by this, on the other to know ourselves at all is to know the truth of it.

So, knowing this, what are we to do? The very question is part of our unchildlikeness: to feel that when we know something to be true we must immediately do something

about it. And Jesus tells us again, "Become like children."
Yet we know that this is impossible. In the very effort of
trying to become like children, if the effort can so much as
be imagined, we put our goal still farther out of reach. But
it is precisely here, perhaps, that we come as near to the heart
of the mystery as we are able. It is just when we realize that
it is impossible by any effort of our own to make ourselves
children and thus to enter the kingdom of Heaven that we
become children. We are children, perhaps, at the very moment when we know that it is as children that God loves
us—not because we have deserved his love and not in spite
of our undeserving; not because we try and not because we
recognize the futility of our trying; but simply because he has
chosen to love us. We are children because he is our father;
and all our efforts, fruitful and fruitless, to do good, to speak
truth, to understand, are the efforts of children who, for all
their precocity, are children still in that before we loved him,
he loved us, as children, through Jesus Christ our Lord.

The Miracles at Hand

And behold, a lawyer stood up to put him to the test, saying, "Teacher, what shall I do to inherit eternal life?" He said to him, "What is written in the law? How do you read?" And he answered, "You shall love the Lord your God with all your heart, and with all your soul, and with all your strength, and with all your mind; and your neighbor as yourself." And he said to him, "You have answered right; do this, and you will live."

But he, desiring to justify himself, said to Jesus, "And who is my neighbor?" Jesus replied, "A man was going down from Jerusalem to Jericho, and he fell among robbers, who stripped him and beat him, and departed, leaving him half dead. Now by chance a priest was going down that road; and when he saw him he passed by on the other side. So likewise a Levite, when he came to the place and saw him, passed by on the other side. But a Samaritan, as he journeyed, came to where he was; and when he saw him, he had compassion, and went to him and bound up his wounds, pouring on oil and wine; then he set him on his own beast and brought him to an inn, and took care of him. And the next day he took out two denarii and gave them to the innkeeper, saying, 'Take care of him; and whatever more you spend, I will repay you when I come back.' Which of these three, do you think, proved neighbor to the man who fell among the robbers?" He said, "The one who showed mercy on him." And Jesus said to him, "Go and do likewise." Luke 10:25–37 RSV

THERE IS a popular television program called *Candid Camera.* It consists of film taken by a crew of cameramen who rove around the country setting up their equipment in hidden places and taking movies of people who have no idea that they are even being watched. The object, as they put it, is to catch people in the act of being people, and the results are sometimes very funny and sometimes quite sad, and once in a while you get the feeling that you have seen something significantly true about human nature in general, including your own. You are apt to get this feeling especially when they turn their hidden cameras on people in the act of witnessing miracles.

One of these miracles, as I remember it, involved the rigging up of a bird cage so that the little hanging perch swang back and forth, and the leaves of some of the plants that they had in it fluttered, and you could hear the bird trilling, and everything was entirely normal except that there was no bird in the cage. Various unsuspecting souls were maneuvered over to it, and the invisible cameras recorded their reactions. Down to the last man, not one of them noticed that anything was wrong. When they were asked what they had been looking at, they all replied that they had been looking at a bird in a cage; and when they were asked to describe what kind of a bird it was, some of them were rather vague, but some of them gave quite detailed descriptions—a yellow beak, a long tail, and so on. In other words, what all of them saw was not what was really there—a cage without a bird in it—but they saw instead what under the circumstances they expected to be there, which was of course a cage with a bird in it.

The other one I remember was very much the same with one significant difference. This time the scene was a perfectly ordinary table in a perfectly ordinary lunchroom, and the only thing that was extraordinary was the flower that was sitting in a vase on the table. Somebody would sit down and start drinking his coffee or his milk or whatever it was, and then when he would set it down for a minute in between sips, the miracle would happen. All of a sudden, the extraordinary flower would rear up out of its vase, arch over, and start inhaling the man's drink. This time, unlike the birdless bird cage, they could not help seeing what was really there—this miraculous flower—but this time they simply refused to come to terms with it. It did not fit in with their conception of reality because their conception of reality excluded the possibility of the miraculous, so what most of them did was just to cast a few furtive glances around to make sure that nobody else had seen and then move away to another table and try to look as if nothing had happened.

These are foolish examples because *Candid Camera* is really a rather foolish kind of affair, but the truth that they point to seems to me to be incontrovertible. Again and again in our lives, all of us tend to mistake what we *see* there for what is *really* there. We see a bird in the cage even though the cage is empty because we expect to see a bird in the cage. And of course the corollary is that we often fail to see what is *un*expected. There are countless examples of this.

Beauty for instance. We expect to see beauty in sunsets and picture galleries and the faces of beautiful people, we expect to hear beauty in the song of a hermit thrush or the Mozart *Requiem*, and it is in these places that we do see beauty and hear it. But of course there is also beauty in the places where we do not expect to find it. We scoop up handfuls of sand from the beach, say, and we see nothing beautiful there—only handfuls of sand. But look at it closely, look again, look so that we begin to see the separate grains, each crystal, and we find that our hands are adorned with splendor. Or we walk down a street, any street, some drab day, and we hear nothing that is beautiful, unless of course we really listen, and then what do we hear? There is the click-clack-click-clack

of our own two feet on the pavement, the sifting of leaves
in the wind, the buzz of a power mower, the barking of a
dog. A ghost would give a thousand years, if he had years to
give, to hear twelve seconds of such blessed music.

We are cursed with language, of course, paralyzed with
words, and that is part of the trouble. Somebody points to
the window and says, "What's that?" And I look to where
he is pointing, and I say, "Why that's the sky. It's just the
sky." I give it a name. I label it. I reduce it to a word that
vaguely suggests all the characteristics that it has in common
with other skies at other times but leaves out all that is unique
about it. And in so doing I dismiss it. I have failed to see
what is really there outside my window and have seen only
my conception of it, my word for it. "Sky" is only a sound I
make with my mouth, after all, a mark I scratch on paper.
What is really there, up there above me now, is not sky. There
is no such thing as sky. It is *that*. It is those fathoms and
fathoms deep of whatever it is, without name or substance or
form. A pair of wings hover in the emptiness of it. It swarms
with light, the stuff and mystery of the universe. "What is
that?" I answer, "Why, it is the sky."

And there are also the things that we see but dismiss because they do not fit into our conception of the way things
are. In the realm of our blindness, we need poets or children
or lunatics to show us the miracles that we do not notice. But
in the realm of our stubbornness, we need scientists. There is
the whole realm of extrasensory perception for instance. For
generations the subject was left to the superstitious and the
fanciful until through the labors of men like Dr. Rhine at
Duke University it began to become a more or less respectable
subject of scientific inquiry, and now people are able not only
to observe such phenomena but to admit that they observe

them. Or dreams. For generations a dream was a dream and nothing more, and anyone who saw it as anything more was called by the educated a crank or a charlatan until the advent of Freud and others. Now we begin to accept a dream for what it more nearly is—a window into the unconscious, a potential source of wisdom and healing. And finally there are the mystics, those men and women who have emerged in every age and every culture bearing their strange tales of encounters with the very source of reality itself. They have called it by different names, of which God is only one, and they have used different kinds of language to describe it; but one way or another, it is clear that they have all experienced the same thing—a peace that passes all understanding, a joy, a power beyond all powers that seeks to reunite men with itself and with each other. But like the man sitting at the table with the drinking flower, we are made uneasy by their troubling presence. We would rather move to another seat and pretend that nothing has really happened. We say that a mystic is a neurotic, as indeed he may be, and there is the end of it. Now back to reality. What will we have for supper tonight? How are we going to deal with the international crisis? But real as such things are, are they all that is real? Are they even the most real kind of real?

The robbers in Christ's parable jumped on the man who was passing by and tore off his clothes and mugged him and left him half dead by the side of the road. After a while a couple of other men came by who were not half dead but only half alive, perhaps, because when they looked at the man lying in the ditch, what they saw, this priest and this Levite, was just a man lying in the ditch. Half dead. And that is apparently all they saw when they looked at him.

They saw the man, of course, but they also saw the road,

and in their mind's eye they saw whatever goal they were traveling that road to reach. Two needs they recognized presumably: the need of the wounded man for help and their own need to get wherever they were going. And let us give them the benefit of the doubt by assuming that it was genuinely important for them to get where they were going and that they felt sure, as was indeed the case, that somebody else would happen along soon anyway. My guess is that they were not especially bad or heartless men, at least no worse or more heartless than anyone reading these words, or writing them, and that is not really so bad, as the world goes. They were just blind men, about as blind anyway as people are usually blind. When they looked at the man in the ditch, all they saw was what people normally expect to see when they look at another person: they saw another person, a self distinct from themselves, a man who had his problems just as they had their problems. And in a sense they were right, of course.

I have my problems, and you have your problems; I have my needs, and you have your needs; and in a sense they really are distinct from each other, and I have to try to decide whose need I am going to try to serve—yours or mine. But to see this is to see only part of what there is to see. To see this is to see only the surface of reality, the expected part. It is like looking at the sand that we scoop up and seeing only the sand, or like gazing up through the window and saying, "SKY."

The reality of it is more than that. As we travel around this world, this life, every man that we meet is the man in the ditch because every man that we meet, no matter how little he looks it and no matter how surprised he might be to realize it, is half dying for need of us—not just of the next person who comes along, though of him too, but of us. In one way or another, every human being is crying out or acting out, or at great cost stifling, his need to be known, accepted, forgiven and healed by us, of all people. So that other self who looks so distinct from ourselves is not quite so distinct after all because he cannot really even *be* a self without us. To be really alive, not just half alive, he needs our help, our healing.

There seems then to be a deeper and more terrible truth still, because to be really alive, not just half alive, we need to help and heal him: his need for mercy is matched by our need to be merciful. It is not just for his sake that we come to his rescue. It is also for our sakes. Neither of us can be really human, really alive, without the other; and every time we pass him by and leave him to his own misery, we both suffer for it. We need each other so infinitely more than we are usually apt to see or to admit that we see.

In Christ's parable, a third man finally did come along, of course. He looked, really looked, and saw not just a man, a man, a man, but saw what was actually sprawled out there in the dust with most of the life whaled out of him. He bound up his wounds, set him on his own beast, took care of him, and his reward was to go down in fame as the *good* Samaritan, which seems to be a marvelously inept title somehow, because just as I prefer to think of the priest and the Levite as less than really bad, more just half blind, in the same way I prefer to think of the Samaritan as more than merely good. I prefer to think that the difference between the Samaritan and the other two was not just that he was more morally sensitive than they were but that he had, as they had not, the eye of a poet or a child or a saint—an eye that was able to look at the man in the ditch and see in all its extraordinary unexpectedness the truth itself, which was that at the deepest level of their being, he and that other one there were not entirely separate selves at all. Not really at all.

Your life and my life flow into each other as wave flows into wave, and unless there is peace and joy and freedom for you, there can be no real peace or joy or freedom for me. To see reality—not as we expect it to be but as it is—is to see that unless we live for each other and in and through each other. we do not really live very satisfactorily: that there can really be life only where there really is, in just this sense, love. This is not just the way things ought to be. Most of the time it is not the way we want things to be. It is the way things are. And not for one instant do I believe that it is by accident that it is the way things are. That would be quite an accident.

It was not a flower at all, of course, the one that leaned its head to drink. It only looked like a flower. In some ways it was such a ludicrous little scene that flickered away on the blue screen, but in another way it was enough to make any-one who has tears for such things weep. A miracle happened —only a very small miracle, but a miracle still. The flower bowed its wild and beautiful head and drank. The man could not avoid seeing it. No one could. He was a dingy, tired-looking man in his shirt sleeves. Life had taught him long ago that there are no miracles in this hard world. But there before his eyes the miracle had happened. So he got up and moved to another place. That would be the point to weep.

As surely as a sailing ship is made to sail with the wind, so are you and I and everybody else in this wide world over made to live bound to each other as a brother is bound to a brother, giving and receiving mercy, binding up each other's wounds, taking care of each other. If we really look at our own lives, seeing not what we expect them to be, but what they are, we cannot help seeing that. Nobody can. It need not have been so. It can be imagined otherwise. We might have been made to live on self-interest or solitude or pure reason. Yet it is so.

So either we get up and move away somewhere, anywhere, as though we had never seen this greatest of all miracles. Or we kiss the flower that bows its head to us, embrace the bright wind that seeks to fill our sails, open our arms, our lives, to the deepest miracle of reality itself and call it by its proper name, which is King of kings and Lord of lords, or call it by any name we want, or call it nothing, but live our lives open to the fierce and transforming joy of it.